Portage: The Importance of Parents

Portage: The Importance of Parents

Proceedings of the Third National Conference on Portage Services at University College, London

Edited by Brian Daly, Jo Addington, Sue Kerfoot and Allan Sigston

NFER-NELSON

Published by The NFER-NELSON Publishing Company Ltd.,
Darville House, 2 Oxford Road East,
Windsor, Berkshire SL4 1DF

and

242 Cherry Street, Philadelphia, PA 19106 – 1906.
Tel: (215) 238 0939. Telex: 244489.

First Published 1985

Library of Congress Cataloging in Publication data

National Conference on Portage Services
(1983: University College, London)
1. Handicapped children – services for – Great Britain – congresses.
2. Handicapped children – Great Britain – family relationships – congresses.
3. Family social work – Great Britain – congresses.
4. Social work with handicapped children – Great Britain – congress.
I. Daly, Brian. II Title.
HV890.G7N38 1983 362.4'088054 85–5089

ISBN 0–7005–0681–0
Code 8188 02 1

Photoset in Plantin by David John Services Ltd, Maidenhead
Printed in Great Britain by A. Wheaton & Co. Ltd, Exeter

Contents

Editorial

Portage is now one of the major success stories, in recent years, of services to young children with special educational needs. Evidence suggests that it is successful because it goes towards meeting some real needs of families with a handicapped child. The Portage phenomenon is also happening in contexts other than homes: in nurseries, in special schools, in residential situations, in day centres and many other settings. As well as producing positive results in these clearly defined areas, other less tangible but nonetheless significant 'spin-offs' are widely reported: parent consumers of Portage home teaching services consistently respond positively to the service offered, and the 'delivery' of a whole range of services to children with special educational needs is being influenced (health visitors, psychologists, speech therapists, occupational therapists, social workers, physiotherapists, etc.) The precise reasons for its success may not be agreed by all who experience it. However, what has undoubtedly helped is the fact that Portage Services are replicable in a wide variety of situations.

In the midst of this exciting diversification it should, nonetheless, be remembered what constitutes a Portage Service:

1. Families are visited weekly at home by a visitor who has completed a Portage Workshop training.
2. The Portage home visitor attends a regular staff meeting with the project supervisor.
3. A checklist is used for initial and on-going assessment.
4. An *activity chart* consisting of instructions, agreed with the parents, on what to teach, how to teach it and what to record, is left with them each week for each of the skills being taught.

5. The agreed teaching procedure is demonstrated by the home visitor (if the visitor cannot do it how can we expect the parent(s) to?!)
6. The home visitor observes the parents carrying out the procedure and offers advice and/or agrees amendments to it.
7. The child's level of skill in the area concerned is recorded both *before* teaching and a week *after* teaching, so that improvements can be measured.
8. There is a management team (of representatives of social services, health, education, voluntary agencies and parents), which meets every three or four months to receive the supervisor's report and deal with related inter-agency or resource issues.

There have been lots of suggested modifications, amendments and additions to the model both in this volume and elsewhere. There are two overriding principles, however, which will influence the acceptance or otherwise of such proposals. The first is the self-critical appeal to *evidence of effectiveness* and the second is an unparalleled commitment to *partnership with parents*.

This volume has come about due to the generous efforts of the contributors who were all involved in making presentations at the Third National Conference in London. This was a very special conference: one in five of the two hundred participants were parents interested in, or receiving, Portage Services. Some of the conference presentations were made by parents too – so the title of the book could not be more apt.

The fact that all presenters to the Conference gave their services completely free and no author fees are involved in this publication, is an indication of the commitment of the contributors to having their views disseminated as widely as possible, amongst professionals and parents alike concerned with young children with special educational needs.

The conference was organized by the Barking and Dagenham Portage Service with much assistance from the Barking and Dagenham Schools' Psychological Service. A big thank you to all those in the Barking and Dagenham area who have helped in any way to make Portage work. There has been tremendous support from the management team, social services, education and health authorities, as well as local councillors and most important of all: parents.

Acknowledgements

This Conference arose out of an invitation received from Tony Dessent, the organizer of the Second National Portage Conference at Cambridge, and we were guided by feedback received from participants there. Nonetheless, in the accountability stakes we are to blame for everything which went wrong!

We are grateful to the following people who also made contributions at the Conference: Dr Jack Singer, Consultant Paediatrician; Kathy East, Chief Speech Therapist; Jan Lloyd and Sue. We were also sorry to hear of the subsequent death of Bernie Spain who presented a seminar paper.

A thank you should go to the staff of Ramsay Hall, University College London who accommodated us and fed us at a very reasonable price. The conference organizers were able to lay on crêche facilities throughout the working days of the conference at no extra charge. In particular we would like to thank Paula Milrose, nursery nurse and her team of student nursery nurses: Janet Bland, Carolyn Richards, Dianne Kindell, Jackie Turner, Donna Carr and Pat Chessell who volunteered their efforts whilst at Havering Technical College doing their NNEB training.

We would also like to thank Bob Hogg, headteacher at Faircross School, Barking for making crêche equipment and toys available.

Chris Mansell did sterling work in the early hours of the Conference helping us to get organized, and shift furniture – thank you, Chris.

Carol Cresswell was invaluable behind the bar which she organized single-handedly – Cheers Carol! Thank you also to the team of volunteers who helped man it and drink it dry!

The credit for the presentation of the best organized conference programme ever seen goes to Sue Rampling, now a secretary with the Barking and Dagenham Schools' Psychological Service. Sue also helped us in a million-and-one other ways in connection with the conference organization in which she was equally efficient.

Particular thanks are due to Geoff Trickey, Principal Educational Psychologist, London Borough of Barking and Dagenham for his support.

Brian Daly
Jo Addington
Sue Kerfoot
Allan Sigston
Conference Organizers and Co-editors
Barking and Dagenham Portage Service

The National Portage Association

This Association has just been set up in order to encourage the growth of Portage Services and to help proper service standards to be maintained. Parent consumers of Portage services are involved at every level: regionally and on each of the executive advisory committees. Membership is open to all parents and professionals who support the broad aims of the Association. Further details concerning membership are available from the regional representatives. [Membership £5 p.a. (£1 for unwaged)]

Regional Representatives

SOUTH WEST	Tim Lister/Steve Huggett Arundel Towers North Portland Terrace Southampton, Hants SO9 4XE
SOUTH EAST AND LONDON	Sue Kerfoot Barking and Dagenham Schools Psychological Service Seabrook House 22 Shipton Close Dagenham, Essex RM8 3QR
MIDLANDS	Barbara McDowell/Christine Dickinson Northampton Schools Psychological Service Springfield Cliftonville, Northants NN1 5BD
EASTERN	Tony Dessent Schools Psychological Service Touthill Close City Road Peterborough PE1 1UJ

NORTHERN	Kath Jennings Child Guidance Clinic Civic Centre High Street Huddersfield HD1 2NE
SCOTLAND	Christine Fitton 77 Lasswade Road Edinburgh EH16 6SZ
IRELAND	Roger Goodliffe School Psychological Service N.E. Education and Library Board County Hall, Galgorm Road Ballmena, Co. Antrim, N. Ireland BT42 1HN
WALES	c/o National Secretary Mollie White King Alfred's College Sparkford Road Winchester, Hants SO22 4NR

International inquiries may be addressed to:

Dee Williams (Chairperson)
National Portage Association
Whitefield School
MacDonald Road
London E17 4AZ

Contributors' addresses

Jan Asplett, Doris Brosnan *et al.*
The Willows Nursery
Battenburg Avenue
Portsmouth

Sue Bendall
Senior Clinical Psychologist
Coleshill Hall Hospital
Gilson Road
Coleshill
Birmingham B46 1DW

Steve Booth
Educational Psychologist
County Educational Psychology Service
High Peak and West Derbyshire Area Education Office
The Crescent
Buxton
Derbyshire SK17 8DJ

Sue Buckley
Senior Lecturer
Department of Psychology
Portsmouth Polytechnic
King Charles Street
Portsmouth PO1 2ER

Jo Cameron
143 Elms Crescent
London SW4

Robert J. Cameron
Educational Psychologist (Training) and Portage Supervisor
Room 235
Department of Psychology
Murray Building
University of Southampton
Southampton

Pamela Courtney
Teacher of Mentally and Visually Handicapped Children
Ellen Terry and Brooklands School
25 Woray Park Road
Reigate
Surrey

Brian Daly
Senior Educational Psychologist/Portage Supervisor
Schools' Psychological Service
Seabrook House
22 Shipton Close
Dagenham RM8 3QR

Bill Gillham
Course Director
Department of Psychology
University of Strathclyde
Turnbull Building
155 George Street
Glasgow G1 1RD

Steve Huggett
Educational Psychologist
Schools' Psychological Service
Battenburg Avenue
North End
Portsmouth PO2 0TA

Tim Jewell
Tutor in Educational Psychology
North East London Polytechnic
Child Study Unit
Psychology Department
The Green
Stratford
London E15

Christine Jones
Portage Home Visitor and Play Therapist
34 Albany Road
Chadwell Heath
Romford
Essex

Clare Jones
Principal Clinical Psychologist
St Cadoc's Hospital
Caerleon
Gwent NP6 1XQ

Albert Kushlick
Research Director HCERT
45–47 Salisbury Road
The University
Highfield
Southampton

Tim Lister
Educational Psychologist
Hampshire Schools Psychological Service
Arundel Towers North
Portland Terrace
Southampton SO9 4XE

Charles Palmer
Educational Psychologist
Coventry School Psychological Service
North Avenue
Stoke Park
Coventry CV2 4DH

Caroline Philps
7 Marion Grove
Woodford Green
Essex

Liz Perkins
District Clinical Psychologist
South Birmingham Health Authority
Oak Tree Lane
Selly Oak
Birmingham B29 6JF

Susan Le Poidevin
Research Psychologist and Tutor in Adjustment to Loss Counselling
3 Bolney Court
Laurie Park Road
London SE26

Philippa Russell
Senior Officer
Voluntary Council for Handicapped Children
National Childrens Bureau
8 Wakely Street
Islington
London EC1 V7QE

Allan Sigston
Educational Psychologist/Portage Supervisor
Schools' Psychological Service
Seabrook House
22 Shipton Close
Dagenham RM8 3QR

John Smith
Research Officer HCERT
45–47 Salisbury Road
The University
Highfield
Southampton

Susan Vicary
Researcher
35 Lancroft Road
London SE22

Mollie White
Lecturer for the Early Years and Member Wessex Portage Team
King Alfred's College
Winchester SO22 4NR

Sheila Wolfendale
Principal Lecturer
North East London Polytechnic
Child Study Unit
Psychology Department
The Green
Stratford
London E15

Introduction

Portage: the Importance of Parents

Brian Daly

Brian Daly is Senior Educational Psychologist and Portage Supervisor with the London Borough of Barking and Dagenham.

The previous book in this series was entitled *What is Important about Portage?* (Dessent 1984) and the title of this book implies one significant answer to that question – parents! For decades research articles and government reports have been leading to the rediscovery of a simple truth:

PARENTS ARE THE BIGGEST SINGLE INFLUENCE ON THE LIVES OF THEIR CHILDREN.

This should not be interpreted to mean that other influences do not matter. Other factors and other people can and do influence the lives of children directly but so too can parents affect and be affected by things around them.

If parents are to be accepted as the major educators of the pre-school child then the *implications* of the fact should also be accepted. Plainly, any service which strives to meet the needs of pre-school children – let alone those who may have special needs – will be firing on one cylinder only if the wishes, desires, competences, values and skills of parents are not fully utilized.

Portage succeeds – and there can be little doubt that it does so (see Tim Lister's chapter in this book) – because it starts where parent and child are and leads on in a direction and in a fashion which fully involves both. There's no doubt that Portage is a robust system, not a set of recipes (see Philippa Russell's chapter later). It responds to the immediate needs of the child, the parent's needs and the prevailing home circumstances. The fact that Portage teaching occurs in the home immediately dismisses one of the biggest problems faced by those involved in skill training at various 'centres of excellence': namely, that of transfer: the difficulties in getting the child to respond appropriately not merely in the context of the nursery/school/clinic/hospital but, more importantly, in real life – at home.

It is clear to me that a home delivery system for pre-school education can be well appreciated and cost effective. When it comes to giving advice for implementation in the home setting, there is nothing like being there.

Support

The words we choose to use are sometimes a matter of personal taste and recently I have started using the word 'handicapped' again. I have been influenced in this decision by the discovery that the word is derived from an old English gambling phrase: 'Hand in cap' used for drawing lots. It seems to me a timely reminder that most difficulties and special needs occur randomly in the population and certainly cannot be blamed on anyone. Nonetheless, powerful feelings are involved. It is often said that the parents of a handicapped child go through a whole set of experiences which other parents do not encounter. There is a sense in which this must be true but there is also a sense in which it is not. Undoubtedly, the parents of a handicapped child have experienced extremely painful feelings in relation to discovering the fact and the implications of their child's condition. However, it is quite another issue to imply that they are therefore 'a race apart'.

Portage services are directed overtly towards educational outcomes and parents state this as being the most valued aspect of the service (See Sue Buckley's chapter). Sean Cameron, in his chapter, reviews data relating to the competences of the parents of handicapped children and amongst his conclusions is that this sub-group of parents is on the whole competent and coping. Parents involved in Portage report that they experience the service – often expressed in terms of a relationship with the Portage home visitor – as 'supportive'. It is indeed a pleasing outcome that this should have been achieved without its being an explicit part of the original Portage model. There must remain considerable doubt, however, that the same sorts of supportive relationships would have been reported if the innermost feelings of the Portage parents had been an explicit target for exploration. In speaking with Portage parents I have been made aware that the message they wish to get across is that Portage is successful precisely because it is practical, non-probing and helps to 'get on with the job'. If, in the process, parents choose to share some of their feelings with the Portage home visitor that is fine, but if they choose not to that is fine too.

One of the parents on our local Portage Project put it very well at one of our parent meetings: *'We're just ordinary people; but perhaps our lows are very low but also our highs can be very high'*.

It's worthwhile to consider some problems posed by support services which focus on the family in the home setting and to contrast these with the benefits of a Portage service, since in so doing the uniquely positive features of Portage are accentuated. If services are to respond to the needs of families of pre-school handicapped children they should be encouraged to *listen* to what parents are saying. I am going to illustrate the rest of this chapter with examples of things said to me by parents (not, incidentally, from the area in which I now work) in order to emphasize the needs to which a Portage service responds.

Practicalities

> *...they were very kind and helped me a lot to accept the fact that I have a handicapped child. That's fine, as far as it goes, but now I want to know what to do about it.*

This parent had accepted the *fact* of her child's handicap, in the sense that she now accepted that it could not be changed and the little girl in question would always have Down's Syndrome. The mother now wished to face up to the *implications* of that fact. It is to be expected that accepting or adjusting to the implications is a much harder and more painful experience than accepting the fact only. It is likely that such adjustment is never completed; there will still be painful parental adjustments to make even when the child grows to an adult. Portage has a useful role in the early period of adjusting to the implications of a child's handicap since it helps to expose the truth of the situation, which is always an *interaction* between what the child brings to the world and the planning and implementation of optimum learning environments. Portage is no panacea, but at least it is addressing real problems in a way which is acceptable to parents and child alike.

Bad news

> *I was told he wouldn't sit up until at least a year old – how did they know that? What could I do to help him? Nobody answered me.*

This parent was refusing to accept the passive parental role sometimes ascribed to the parents of handicapped children by professionals. The prediction business is fraught with difficulties but there are predictions which can be made about certain conditions. However, it is also true to say that the actions of the immediate care givers can and do make a significant contribution to the development of all handicapped children. Both sides of the story should be given. I am sure that someone with the empathic skill of Susan Le Poidevin (a contributor to this volume) would perform such a task in an exemplary fashion. There is no doubt that breakers of bad news require preparation and training since too many parents reach Portage schemes with a string of horror stories concerning bad news givers.

Generalities

> *They told us general things like 'talk to him more often' but nothing specific like how to get him to call his sister by her name.*

Perhaps you will have seen the poster in health centres and clinics which depicts a mother holding a baby up to her face and talking. 'Ga Ga means talk to me', is printed across it. It is obviously sound advice that any care-giver (not just the mother) should talk to young babies. However, such advice is very general and leaves far too many questions unanswered – especially for the parent of a handicapped child.

- What should be said to the child?
- What response is being sought?
- What should be done when the response is made?
- What should be done when the response isn't forthcoming?

Portage has a great strength in its specificity and any Portage activity would include the answers to these questions. There is undoubtedly a need to make advice-givers accountable for formulating their advice in clear unambiguous language instead of hiding behind generalities.

Unwanted behaviours

> *We were given some very useful advice concerning teaching her new things but nothing at all which was realistic about coping with her bizarre behaviour.*

This parent was in receipt of a peripatetic home teaching service to partially hearing children. Services to the hearing impaired were the first in the county to realize formally the potential of home teaching. Now many teachers of the hearing impaired are taking Portage principles on board and are being even more effective. Portage services recognize that interfering behaviours, such as rocking, headbanging and so on need to be tackled before it is possible to plan realistically for helping with other developmental deficits. Portage deals with problem behaviour in a systematic way which depends on careful record keeping and consistent management.

Weekly at home

> *She gave us some very useful tips, but we didn't have the chance to come back to her when things went wrong...*

This parent went on to explain that there was a three-month waiting list to get another appointment at the hospital. The parent and the professional were suffering from an inappropriate 'delivery system'. Portage aims to overcome such problems by being there each week and having access to some professional guidance through the supervisor and management team. It's clearly not a matter of saying that every service which operates on an appointment or waiting list system is ineffective, but rather concluding that Portage has some real advantages for planning, implementing and monitoring home-focused activities. Many Portage schemes use the advice of rarely seen professionals and are able to provide very valuable data to such professionals in order to evaluate outcomes.

Parent partnership

> *Imagine how terrible I felt when I found out he had been eating with a spoon and fork at the nursery for over a year, and yet he never does at home.*

This parent's discovery is not unusual – much early learning is context bound. What is manifested here is a lack of communication between nursery and home and a consequent lack of cooperative endeavour in helping the child generalize his newly acquired skill. Many nurseries and special nurseries now use the Portage model to good effect in jointly planning activities with parents from the outset, thus harnessing previously untapped potential and directing all efforts in a coordinated cooperative fashion.

In her chapter later on in the book Sheila Wolfendale examines in some detail the concept of parental involvement and parent/professional partnership. It seems to me that Portage offers a very effective forum for, firstly, *listening* to each other and, secondly, jointly *planning* and then *carrying out* activities designed to help the young handicapped person.

Parent power is not always at its most effective when used in an adversarial way: in conflict with the service administrators. Neither is professional power most effectively used when seemingly justifying and accepting the status quo. Portage services are rightly proud of the very productive way that parents and professionals work together. Portage presents a model for parent/professional partnership resulting in outcomes which are many times more effective for the child than those obtained by merely adding the respective skills together.

Beginners' Portage

Allan Sigston

Allan Sigston is an educational psychologist and Portage supervisor with the London Borough of Barking and Dagenham.

The intention of this paper is to give a brief description of Portage for those whose knowledge is partial or incomplete.

Portage is a system intended to help parents to teach their handicapped child at home on a daily basis. It involves a trained home visitor calling on the family on a weekly basis and working with parents and child. During this visit the home visitor and parent(s) agree on new skills which they would like the child to learn and agree on teaching activities that will be carried out daily by the parent in order to achieve them. The Portage home visitors are trained through an intensive 3-day Workshop and are supervised by a Project supervisor.

Portage began in Wisconsin in 1969 as a response to the problem of providing an educational service to pre-school handicapped children in a large rural area. However, since that time and its adoption in the UK in 1976, its appeal has rested upon its success in meeting a number of common problems voiced by parents about services generally supplied to families of handicapped children. Professionals involved with providing such services will probably be familiar with some of these points.

Many parents have reported that in the past services have not met their wishes for practical advice as to teaching their child new skills or for dealing with difficult behaviours. Frequently mentioned has been the over-generality of advice; for instance, 'talk to him more often' rather than specific information. One of the most common concerns for parents has been the infrequency of meetings with professionals, so that where practical advice has been forthcoming a long time may elapse before it is possible to get help on the next step when things have been successful, or resolving a problem that has arisen when things have gone wrong.

The relative success of Portage in reducing these difficulties would seem to be the main cause of its rapid growth in this country and elsewhere, in rural and urban settings often very different from its origins. This success seems to be based on two particular key components which are the Structured Teaching Technique and the Positive Monitoring System.

The Structured Teaching Technique

As has been described, each week a home visitor and parent will agree on at least one goal to be achieved in the coming week, in conjunction with an activity that will be carried out daily. Both of these are summarized on the Activity Chart, an example of which is shown in Fig. 1. This always includes a number of common elements, the first of which is a teaching target which describes the behaviour we wish the child to show in order to demonstrate successful learning; a criterion level will also be set, indicating the success rate we wish the child to achieve in relation to the number of learning trials carried out in the course of the day.

The teaching activity will include details of where it will happen, the apparatus required and what the parent will do and say. There are two crucial procedures in addition to this; the first is known as the Success Procedure and consists of a reward that will be given immediately after the child has carried out the target behaviour. The second is the Correction Procedure, which is what will happen if the child fails to respond or responds incorrectly and this will involve giving the child some *additional* help to ensure that he or she completes the task successfully. This will be coupled with a mild reward.

Great importance is placed on recording the child's attempts in order that the effects of teaching can be appropriately assessed. At the beginning of the week the home visitor will model the activity as described on the activity chart and then observe the parent carrying it out. This then gives a measure of the child's starting point (known as the baseline) as well as ensuring that the parent and home visitor both fully understand the activity. Similarly, at the end of the week, first the parent and then the home visitor will carry out the activity in order to see how the child performs after teaching (known as the post baseline) and this can then be compared to the level of success hoped for in the teaching target. The parent will also keep a daily record of the child's attempts.

Figure 1 Activity chart

N/Att ______ CHECKLIST NO. (if any) Motor [illegible] CHILD'S NAME Ben

Sus ______ Date of start of activity 30/10/81 HOME VISITOR'S NAME Sue Kerfoot

Ad ______

Contd ______

PA ______

Crit Day Att 6

Contd ______

PA ______

C/L item att ______

Target Behaviour: (include any PROMPTS used)

Ben will stand up from sitting in a chair with physical aid

Criterion: 4/4 Practise 4 times each day

Directions:

Place: Lounge, Ben sat in his chair

What Parent does/says:

Kneel in front of Ben and place your forefingers in his hands to grip and say, "Stand up Ben."

Time limit: 5 seconds

	Baseline										Post Baseline	
	HV	P									P	HV
4	(✓)	✓	✓	✓	✓	✓	✓	✓	✓		✓	✓
3	✓	✓	(✓)	(✓)	✓	(✓)	✓	✓	✓		✓	✓
2	(✓)	(✓)	(✓)	✓	✓	(✓)	✓	✓	✓		✓	✓
1	✓	(✓)	✓	(✓)	(✓)	✓	(✓)	✓	✓		✓	✓

Days .... T F S S M T W ....

How to record: ✓ Ben stands up without extra help
(✓) Ben stands up when pulled by mum

Success Procedure: Hugs, kisses and say, "Good Boy Ben!"

Correction Procedure: Say again, 'Stand up Ben,' and pull on your forefingers until he stands, then say, 'Good Boy Ben'

The Positive Monitoring System

This ensures the consistent delivery of the Portage service to homes while allowing access to relatively scarce professional advice and an ability to collaborate in the solving of problems. Although there are some variations between Portage services, generally speaking the same format applies.

The supervision group:

Regular meetings (usually weekly or fortnightly) are attended by the home visitors together with a nominated supervisor. Here the week's successes will be shared as will problems in achieving weekly teaching targets or other problems that may have been raised by the family. Usually children will be considered in turn with regard to the setting of long-term targets (three – four months ahead) to be agreed between the family and home visitor. Often other specialists, such as physiotherapists, will attend to give advice on teaching programmes.

The management team:

The supervisor of the supervision group will then report back, usually three or four times a year, to the management team consisting of representatives of agencies concerned with the welfare of families receiving the Portage service. As well as providing an overview of the effectiveness of the project, this group would also consider queries relevant to their agencies as well as the staffing and funding of the project.

While this arrangement is robust enough to accommodate changes of personnel at any level without causing a great disruption to the services delivered to families, it can also be flexible in meeting the changing needs of the population it serves.

The Portage materials

Two invaluable aids available to the home visitor are published by the NFER–NELSON Publishing Company. The first is the *Portage Checklist;* this is divided into six sections titled Infant Stimulation, Socialization, Language, Self-help, Cognitive and Motor. Except for Infant Stimulation, each of these is divided into a hundred or more sequenced items mapping normal child development from birth to approximately five to six years of age. The Checklist is used for initially assessing the child's skills, for recording progress and as a guide to the setting of targets in both the short and long term. The NFER–NELSON Publishing Company have since published the *Wessex Revised Portage Language Checklist* (White and East, 1983), which is a variation on that found in the original.

The other item of great importance is the set of teaching cards. Each of the 580 developmentally sequenced checklist items has a corresponding teaching card which states a number of possible teaching suggestions. While these are not specific enough to transfer directly to an activity chart, they provide a useful resource in suggesting activities that could be suitably adapted.

It will probably also be of interest to the reader that NFER–NELSON also publish a number of books related to the implementation of Portage.

The future of Portage

As you will see from the contributions to this book, there is considerable variation amongst Portage projects. Some are staffed by unpaid volunteers, others involve nursery nurses, psychiatric nurses, teachers, physiotherapists and a range of other professionals. Some Portage workers are employed by Health Authorities, some by Local Education Authorities and some by the Social Services, many are paid by funds contributed by combinations of these. They are based in schools, hospitals or clinics, some are in Parents' Centres. This rapid growth across professional barriers and different agencies, particularly at a time when finance has been difficult to obtain, speaks volumes for the enthusiasm people feel for Portage, which in turn has led to the establishment of the National Portage Association, which has been set up for the purpose of disseminating information about Portage and promoting its development. Further details can be obtained from the regional representatives listed at the beginning of the book.

Parent Perspectives

Portage – Partnership with Parents

Philippa Russell

Philippa Russell is Senior Officer with the Voluntary Council for Handicapped Children.

It is in the nature of any project, new service or innovation that there should be marked changes over time in the way it is regarded. The initial wave of enthusiasm and sometimes 'unlimited optimism' from those involved in the innovative work which is so vital in initially establishing a project will inevitably give way over time to some questioning and criticism from those who are less involved and less committed. Portage services are not unique in this respect. Portage, like many innovative services, became a 'cult'. 'Doing Portage' and the magic of a package approach for *all* parents became fashionable concepts for any professional working with families with handicapped children. What is important is not that time brought awareness of shortcomings but that those individuals committed to the continuation and further development of innovatory services were able both to take on board and to explore the criticisms of others, and more importantly, to be self-critical. Hence, the theme of the Second National Portage Conference. *What is Important About Portage?* (Dessent, 1984) was a title intended to encourage constructive criticism from those actively engaged in operating parent-centred Portage Services – the belief being that it is possible to be openly critical of a model to which one is highly committed, and that the model can better adjust and develop as a result.

My following remarks concern the evolution of home visiting services, questions to do with parent motivation and the advantages of parental involvement on infant development. I go on to give further consideration to the place of Portage in this crucial area of parent participation particularly in view of recent developments in special education.

Early educational home visiting

Political initiatives in the USA in the 1960s led to a formal recognition that the family was the most effective and economical system for fostering and sustaining the development of a young child. Research indicated the isolation and depression of many young mothers and suggested that successful pre-school education must also involve *adult* education since change in the child would not be effective without corresponding change in the *mother*. The early intervention programmes (which included Portage) were hence:

1. Largely compensatory and non-selective, including all children in a given and usually socially deprived area.
2. Directed at children as early as possible, since Levenstin and Bronfenbrenner's conclusion is that early home visiting was associated with least 'wash out' later in school.
3. The *partnership* with the home visitor or educator was seen as an integral part of the success – not least because it could act as a change agent in relationships to professionals like teachers and psychologists later encountered in the child's life.
4. The programme taught success to mothers who often felt dismal failures on every level. Their active contribution in enhancing their child's linguistic and cognitive development could be seen as *their* success.
5. Such programmes clearly demonstrated that many mothers (particularly the socially deprived) were unaware that young children needed to be *taught* certain skills. Such parents frequently lacked skills in play and could not create a spontaneous play or learning situation without *demonstration*.

Current educational home visiting

Recent developments in home visiting here and in the USA have seen a twofold thrust:

(a) Educational home visiting aimed at linking parent and child to a school-based service (i.e., preparation for formal education). In this context the visitors will usually be educational professionals.

(b) Voluntary schemes are often linked up with education services but frequently are more involved in *self-help* and general support and counselling. Visitors are often former clients and volunteers.

Geoff Poulton (1974) noted that all schemes, whether school-based or independent, had certain common factors.

1. They placed great emphasis on initial visit and mutual trust.
2. Usually a contract would be drawn up, defining the limits of the visitor's work and the amount of time which the parent would give to the scheme.
3. The parents understood their right to withdrawal from the scheme.
4. The scheme usually began with the visitor's introducing activities to the *child* and gradually involving the mother who would become involved in direct teaching during and in between visits.
5. Since the schemes were geared to self-help, parents were encouraged to help themselves. A common problem of most schemes was that of giving help to the full-time working parents.

The schemes all seemed to produce certain common denominators.

1. They indicated the strong link between social and educational needs, since most parents use the visitors for other help.
2. They demonstrated to the educators what very real pressures many parents had to labour under. For example, a drop-off in educational progress might be due to competing anxieties about a strike at the local pit, or a threatened eviction.
3. All the parents seemed to indicate clearly that they were willing to accept a considerable part in the responsibility for educating their children (the survey showed 70%).

Studies by the Hester Adrian Research Centre and others suggest that the *type* of educational material needed by parents may vary. Parents who have received further education may be better able to learn from lectures or reading materials, whilst those without may need more *demonstration and discussions*. However, the *level* of education bore no relationship to the long-term results of the child.

The same studies suggest that some parents may need considerable help in accepting their child's handicap. Denial is common and recent research suggests that many parents have not in fact fully accepted their child's disability a year after birth. There is some evidence that parents of lower intellectual groups find mental handicap less disturbing than those who find their own value systems challenged. The prevalance of denial is born out by Wolfensberger and Kurtz (1974) who found that only 42 per cent of a sample of parents with mental handicap actually admitted that their child was mentally retarded – though they did admit to language delay and other problems. As Dr Rubissow of Honeylands noted, it is tricky beginning work with families who have not yet acknowledged there is a problem. Many schemes do not include some families yet adjustment to acceptance may be a critical need.

Parent motivation

All parents need some time and opportunity to talk through their feelings before being asked to participate in a programme. Such discussions can be of exceptional value in ensuring that parent motivation is strong, and might usefully raise any or all of the following points.

1. *Contingency planning or the contract:* early research by Shearer and others has consistently shown that a contract basis works. First, the parents are clear about the level of undertaking. Second, they are aware that they must participate in order to continue (although exclusion is rare). Third, early success encourages ongoing participation.

2. *Parents need to be given skills* to help them solve their own problems. *Over-dependence* on therapists or home visitors is always a threat and never productive. Some parents, however, go the other way and reject *home-based* intervention programmes, because they wish their child to have *expert* treatment.

3. *Support from other professionals* Some parents might have a deep suspicion of health visitors, social workers and so on. The growth of domiciliary services (peripatetic teachers for the deaf, home visitors, social workers, home liaison teachers etc.) can be confusing and daunting.

4. *Planned success* is the integral factor for many families. However, parents need to be helped to see that the relative ease of many early stages of a home intervention programme does not indicate failure if they subsequently encounter problems with a period of 'no growth'. Hence planned success needs to take into account not only immediate contingency activities but also long-term objectives.

5. *Training or education?* Sometimes the purpose of an activity is not clear. Should parents teach their children? Training is primarily concerned with the mastery of *skills* and does not necessarily require that the user questions the rationale of the training. The distinction, as Cliff Cunningham notes (1982), is that education is aimed at the needs of the learner, not those of the parent or attendant. Parents may need help in giving both *choice* and *exploration* to a handicapped child and helping that child acquire skills which are socially acceptable.

6. *Who else can work with the child?* Identifying additional people who might be able to contribute to the child's development in some way can be useful. The new growth in early intervention programmes has extended their application to other care-givers; for example, staff in day nurseries; residential care staff, child minders and so on. Indeed, one of the questions that has to be asked with regard to early intervention is 'Should parents be allowed to opt out?' The level of involvement may vary according to other family needs and certain dangers in expecting parents to be too good parents.

The effect of parent support on the developing infant

What advantages do we look for?

1. General Early Home Visiting programmes tend to judge success by improvement in morale and general satisfaction of the *mother*. (Burden, 1978).

2. *What difference does it make to the children?* Early Home Visiting (EHV) programmes suggest that early *intervention* generally enhances cognitive and social skills and that the children do appear to do better in school. The earlier the intervention, the less the loss after starting school.

3. Merely observing *regular assessment* seemed to give parents ideas and to encourage more purposeful interaction. Modelling can be a powerful training device for parents of mentally handicapped children.

4. Brinkworth (1975) and de Coriat *et al.* (1968) similarly demonstrate a significant difference in IQ between children of those parents enrolled in educational programmes from the *child's birth onwards* and those left alone to 'spontaneous evolution'.

5. How much is enough? The Hester Adrian Research Centre found that children visited fortnightly did not differ greatly from those visited every six weeks. However, the *parents* would have liked more frequent visits. Parents seemed to learn as much from the informal end part of the visit as from the more structured earlier part.

Why Portage?

Principles not recipes

One of the early dangers of the Portage model was that its 'little blue box' led to its being seen as a universal cookbook for improving the performance of a handicapped child and offering instant teaching skills to the parents. Many of the early schemes literally 'bought' Portage and saw its strict application as being sufficient in itself.

There is no doubt that parents need training in order to work more effectively with children who may present professionals with quandaries and unanswered questions when considering problem solving and longer term development. Indeed, as the Warnock Report noted, parents must be key people in ensuring that *professional* intervention is truly effective and shared goals and an understanding of the strategies for meeting them must now be an integral part of professional support. Portage at its best offers parents the opportunity to understand the *principles* behind any intervention rather than offering, like a car care manual, recipes for tightening belts and guaranteeing better performance. As Elizabeth Newson has often said, parents *are* experts on their own child. They have a rich and unique knowledge of how that child functions and of his or her abilities and disabilities. But they may not know how to organize the knowledge in a way which is directly relevant to helping the child. Indeed that knowledge *without* the help of a professional may actually hinder parents in helping, since it may make the situation appear depressing, confusing and hopeless.

Parental involvement in assessment has grown in the last decade and the majority of families are told much more by many more professionals than was true for parents of my generation. This in turn may produce problems. Many assessments are inevitably *negative*. They outline deficits in children who are already not achieving. Parents not surprisingly want assessment to be *predictive*, sometimes of progress which can never be achieved. The mother who recently suggested that her child's assessment was like 'failing your MOT – even the brakes were faulty' expressed what Portage can avoid.

The strengths of Portage are that:

a) it *must* utilize what the parents already know

b) it *must* involve a caring and trained home visitor who is able to link back to a wider network of professionals

c) it is a *private* service in as much as it can take place in a venue chosen by the parents. Successes and failure need not be displayed prematurely before a wide range of professionals who could be perceived as judging the parents

d) the parents can select priorities for the children which are compatible with their own life-styles. *Educational* goals in terms of cognitive development may be less important (and indeed unattainable) than more immediate, practical problems unless the parents have first overcome these problems (like difficult behaviour)

e) the actual level of parental involvement can be matched to individual family dynamics. In a real world the mother of three pre-school children, living in poor housing and depressed by marital problems, is unlikely to be able to participate as actively as a young couple with few other commitments, time, a good home environment and an enthusiastic attitude to working with their child. *Portage, at its best, avoids overloading the system.* And since it is home-based, parents do not need to compare themselves surreptitiously with each other.

Parent variables

The last few years have seen increasing criticism – or questioning – of Portage and its application. Many criticisms reflect, probably correctly, some of the earlier relatively ill-considered and rigid applications of the approach. Portage cannot exist in a vacuum. A specific task-orientated curriculum must be put in the broader context of parents' other needs and must be backed by general supportive services.

The Honeylands Home Therapy Scheme (Pugh, 1981), a home visiting scheme for parents of severely handicapped children up to two years old, found that many parents were incapable of working systematically with their children until they had been able to resolve their own problems and depression. Hence an early task of a Portage Home Visitor, like the Honeylands Home Therapist, may be to work with the parents in resolving *their* difficulties: in identifying the major problem areas (which may lie in self-care skills, play, behaviour and other specific areas as well as in broader developmental terms) and acting as an *honest broker*.

If parents are not fully aware of the implications of their child's disability and, indeed, if they deny the existence of any problems, any early intervention programme is likely to have minimal success.

One early concern about Portage and, indeed, other Home Teaching Initiatives, was that it might by implication teach parents that if by altering *their* behaviour, they could alter the *child's* behaviour, then it was only a small step for parents to say therefore the problem was theirs in the first place – and more importantly – to believe that they had failed in not making their child 'normal' (Yule, 1975).

The Honeylands Home Therapists programme clearly demonstrated that parents needed to be helped to resolve their own feelings and needs before they could work constructively with their child. In this context the success of Portage will also lie in its ability to take a retrospective as well as prospective assessment of parents' and children's needs.

Portage, however, has a number of checks. The home visitor will be familiar and well known to the family. She or he is also part of a wider network of services which can in turn monitor progress.

Portage works towards planned success, with long-term goals. It also permits modification of these goals with the agreement of the parent. It offers a *self-help* orientation without judgement and does not preclude the wider network of contact, which might involve parents' groups, participation in other programmes (for example, with speech therapists or physiotherapists), and contact with other professionals (such as the peripatetic teacher for the deaf).

If Portage has been criticized for being primarily an *educational* approach to early intervention, it should be remembered that early education not only *can* begin at 0 years under the 1981 Education Act 1981, but that much early education in the past has been heavily institution-based and has actually excluded parents, often by default because of travel and other problems.

Limitations

Portage, like any other intervention scheme, cannot be a universal panacea. Portage myths abound, as Tony Dessent demonstrated at the last Portage conference. Not everybody can be a good home teacher. Professional skills are not enough and personality, the ability to empathize and – working in the home – personal chemistry are all important.

Success requires:

a) a thorough knowledge of the approach used;
b) some basic knowledge of child development;
c) a knowledge of resources within the community;
d) an understanding of relationships;
e) a careful consideration of the ethics of intrusion.

Again – whatever type of intervention programme – the home workers need support. Many will be required to work in environments utterly alien to their own housekeeping or work standards. As Sandow and Clark (1981) described, the problems of working in 'a room 12 by 8 with four generations of hostile family in an atmosphere redolent of fish and chips and cigarette smoke' are considerable.

Early intervention programmes for families with handicapped children

Undoubtedly the proliferation of schemes for families of deprived children – that is, *compensatory* home visiting programmes – influenced the new move to working with families of *handicapped* children at the same time that a range of studies and reviews of the use of the application of behaviour modification principles to childhood disorders stimulated interest in training parents to modify their children's behavioural disorders effectively.

The application of behaviour modification to parent training continues to grow, although a number of research reviews criticize the lack of controls and evaluation and particularly the failure to generalize from such modification techniques and define training variables.

Such training variables might include:

a) the use of group discussions;
b) the need for comparative investigations of programme techniques;
c) lectures and demonstrations, modelling techniques;
d) a better understanding of parent variables.

However, criticisms apart, O'Dell wrote in 1974 that: 'Like many applied areas of behaviour modification, parent training is being quickly expanded by the vacuum of need.'

The Hester Adrian Research Centre's parent involvement project

All home intervention schemes must therefore recognize individual (albeit often temporary) problems such as the following.

1. Outside pressures on the family such as redundancy, illness or marital problems.

2. Temporary family difficulties such as a new baby, job or minor sickness.

3. A preference initially for the child to be treated *outside* the family. Working in the family may require preparation and counselling.

4. The need for the *child* to be temporarily removed from the family either to alleviate stress or because the parents may be experiencing particular difficulties with a problem. Such a removal, to a playgroup, child developmental centre or other form of care, does not mean that a home-based learning service cannot be introduced either in addition to or after the other provision. Portage may complement other services.

In conclusion

Portage offers a flexible approach to helping children through their parents. It reinforces parental competence by teaching success. It also introduces parents to concepts of development which are applicable in a broader context, for example, it ensures parents' participation in the assessment procedures relating to the Education Act, 1981.

An initial problem arising from the wide and growing enthusiasm for Portage is its application without attention to the supervision, self-monitoring and carefully structured support which is part of the Portage approach. 'Doing Portage' is sometimes misinterpreted as possession of the kit, and success may lead to well motivated but inadequate innovations. The Education Act, 1981 is likely to lead to a growth in provision for the 0–5s. Such provision is likely to emphasize parental involvement and Portage offers a proven, low-cost and flexible model for service development.

The decision to form a National Portage Association is an important step forward in underlining credibility, and also ensuring 'minimum standards'. Portage is an important resource, but in the last resort its wider application will depend on acceptable standards and professional and parental satisfaction. Recent questioning of the validity of the approach reflects not dissatisfaction but rather a more informed awareness of the potential and hence of the hazards. Partnerships are never easy but the Portage model offers a framework for the collaboration between parents and professionals which must be a central theme of the 1981 Education Act.

Parental Role in Portage: a consumer view

Caroline Philps and Christine Jones

Caroline Philps is the mother of a Down's Syndrome child. Christine Jones is a Portage home visitor working in the London Borough of Barking and Dagenham.

(This paper is a summary of the use of the Portage Project with a Down's Syndrome child from the age of six weeks to two years. It discusses the changes in approach felt necessary during that period and the pattern of development that emerged as shown by the dates when checklist items were attained. It is a joint account written by parent Caroline Philps and home visitor Christine Jones.)

The parent's account

Elizabeth, our first child, was born with Down's Syndrome in April 1981. Shortly after her birth I was contacted by the local Down's Group, who told me about the Portage Project which had recently begun in our area. At the baby clinic I discovered that Chris was willing to become our home visitor. She was a nursery nurse working in the local play therapy group.

I had read of the need for early stimulation of Down's children if they were to fulfil their potential. I had read books full of ideas. But there is a big gap between knowing of the need to stimulate one's child and actually implementing a daily programme. The practical, detailed daily instructions and record sheet that Portage provides bridged this gap for me. It helped to dispel my early feelings of helplessness and some of the depression of the early months of adjusting to life with a handicapped child. It was good to have something concrete to do daily to help my child. It was good to start when Elizabeth was six weeks old when these feelings were strong, and it was a great encouragement to have a weekly visit from someone especially interested in the problems that my child presented.

My expectations

I expected that we would be able to help Elizabeth to learn new skills. I wonder if I hoped too to make her into a normal child if we tried hard enough. Perhaps there is a danger with a successful programme of seeing it as the answer to the problem rather than a means to alleviate some of the effects.

When Elizabeth was about five months old I was able to attend a Portage training course. I found this helped me to understand the methodology of the project. It was helpful to learn how to break tasks down into teachable fragments and to work towards long-term goals. With Elizabeth I found that long-term goals helped me to look at the future more confidently, taking the pressure off the present and the sometimes slow progress made.

Our approach and the way it changed through time

At the start Elizabeth's progress seemed very close to the normal and we rushed to tick off checklist items. Perhaps this was partly to prove to myself that Elizabeth was not very badly handicapped. This resulted in our choosing activities that were sometimes too hard for her and we spent a long time practising before we achieved our goal. This may have caused Elizabeth to become frustrated.

At the National Portage Conference in 1982 I was impressed by a seminar by Mollie White about the Wessex Language checklist (White and East, 1984) in which she suggested the need to practise early listening skills which might come at the beginning of the checklist. She also said it was important to practise skills in several different contexts and to keep on practising, even some time after the skills were achieved. If someone had suggested going back and practising skills that Elizabeth had learnt at the beginning of the Portage programme, soon after we had started, I would have seen this as a failure because of the need at the start to press on forwards. As I relaxed and began to understand Portage better I was willing to be more flexible and realistic in my thinking.

The need to use skills in a variety of contexts (generalization), underlined at the conference, helped me to see how Portage could be of value in all areas of Elizabeth's development. She needed different kinds of play experience, all teaching the same concept; for example, posting shapes in a shape sorter, matching lids to saucepans (toy ones or real), fitting in Jigsaw pieces, posting letters; all teaching concepts of shape matching. Dressing and feeding could also become learning experiences, skills to be taught by modelling and prompting. I began to experience Portage not just as 20 minutes of activities each day but as a framework upon which to build the many activities that go to make up the baby's or toddler's day.

Problems encountered

1. Judging early long-term goals

From the age of six weeks to 18 months it was often difficult to know in which area to set long-term goals to judge the rate of development. This became less difficult as it gradually became obvious that for a few months Elizabeth would concentrate on motor activities and then she might move into a cognitive or language phase. It became easier to recognize the pattern of development that emerged and to select activities that fitted into it as time passed. (See Figure 1.)

2. The language checklist

The jumps in development needed between each item on the checklist were too great to enable us to set meaningful activities to achieve the items. The Wessex Revised Language checklist came to our aid by filling in the gaps with more items on comprehension, which Elizabeth finds much easier to achieve, and by linking up all the items on the whole checklist that include language work.

A practical aid to language work during the first two years with Elizabeth was to record every sound made in the early days and then every word as these began slowly to occur. This was both encouraging and informative as we tried to link this in with the work done by Bill Gillham on the first words children speak and how to encourage language development from these (see Bill Gillham's paper in this book). Since her second birthday we have found the Makaton vocabulary (Walker 1980) a fine encouragement to Elizabeth to try and express herself.

3. The sequence of checklist items

At the start of the Portage Project we assumed the need to follow the order of the checklist as to the activities to be carried out. As time passed it became obvious that Elizabeth was not going to complete items in this set order. Some items were completed at the same time, especially in the cognitive area, while in Motor Development Elizabeth sometimes completed items much earlier than expected while the next one on the list might be delayed for months.

In order to deal with this problem we developed greater flexibility. We decided to practise all the activities on the list in the section for between one and two years simultaneously, in a kind of ascending spiral of difficulty for the weekly tasks. This provided variety for Elizabeth who was easily bored by repeated activities and it meant

Figure 1: Patterns of development

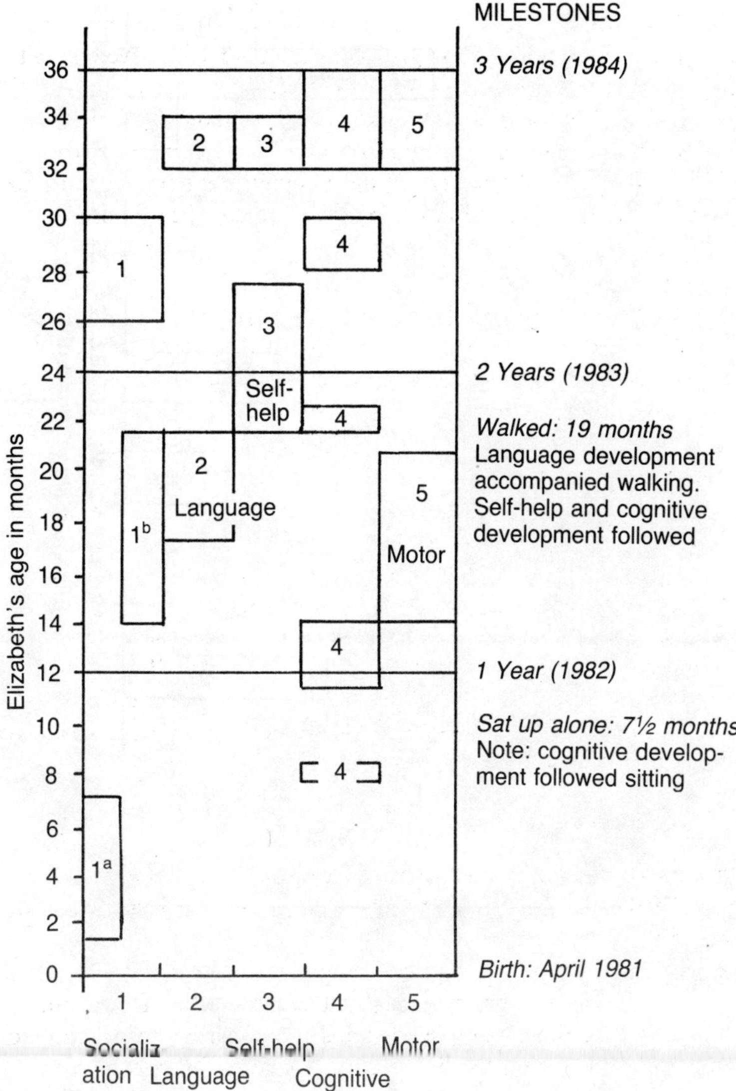

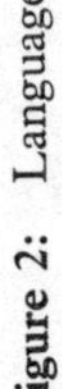

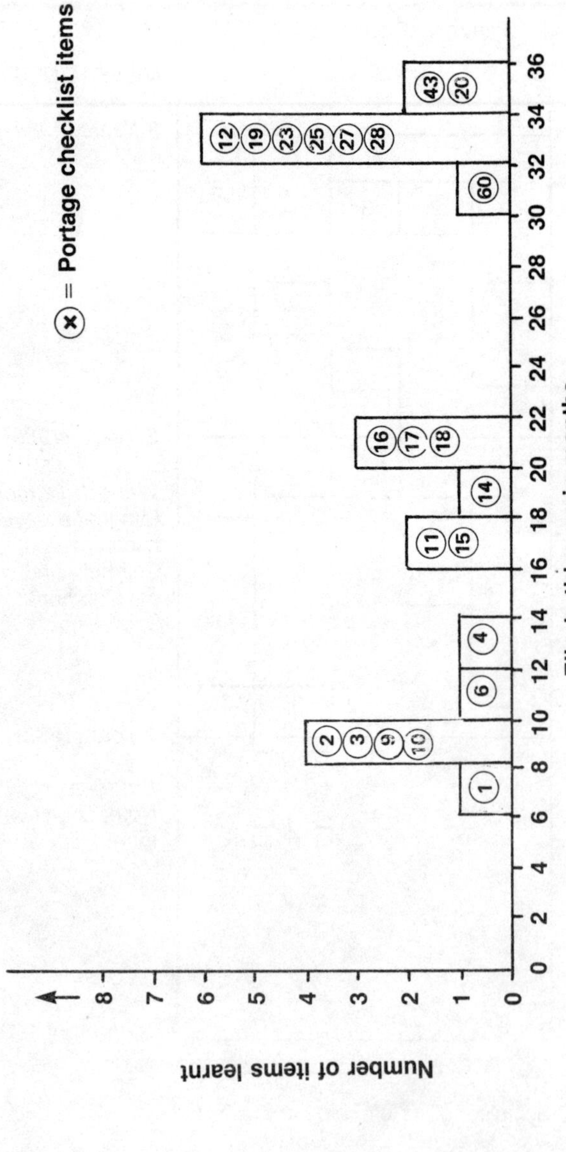

Figure 2: Language

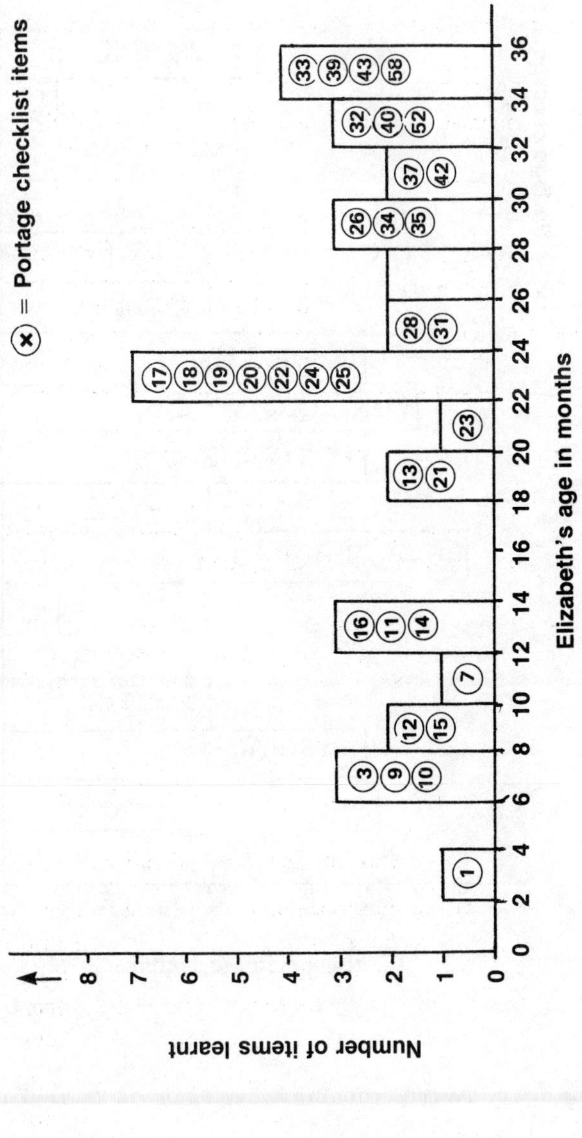

Figure 3: Cognitive

ⓧ = Portage checklist items

Number of items learnt

Elizabeth's age in months

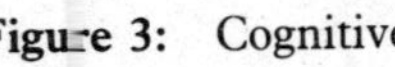

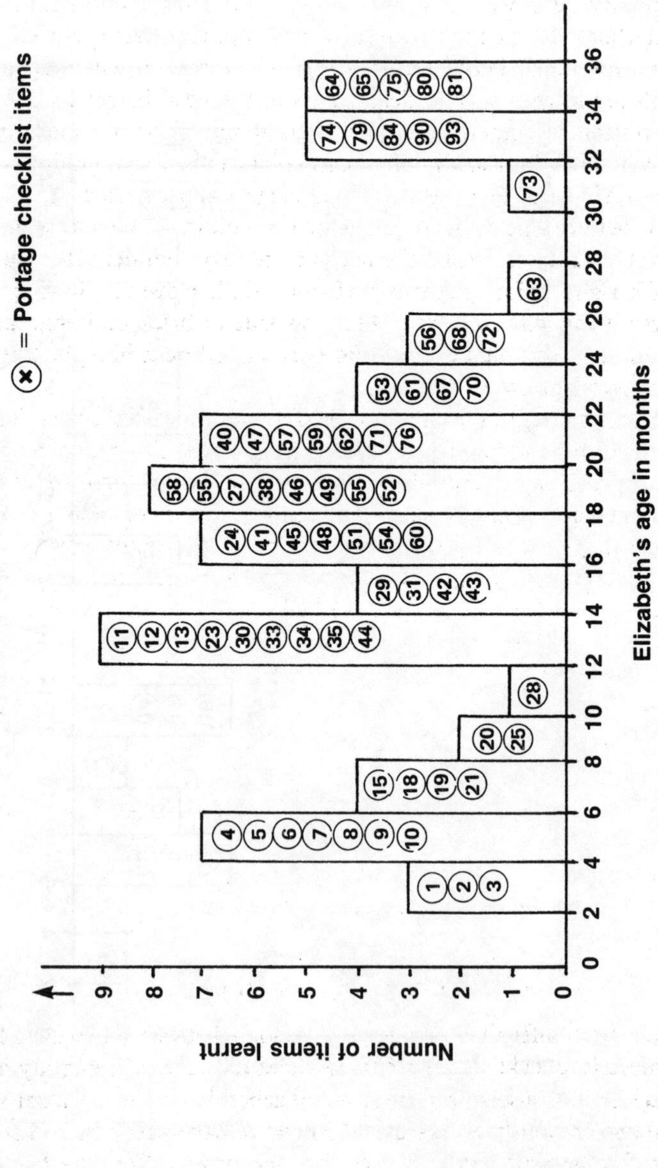

Figure 4: Motor

that we could capitalize on the fact that many of the skills were emerging at the same time and seemed to be naturally linked.

In fact Elizabeth achieved seven out of the ten cognitive skills in February 1983 when she was one year and ten months old. This underlines the stepped pattern of development that occurred with cognitive skills. Perhaps this is due to the way in which cognitive skills are learnt. A great deal occurs in the head before its physical expression is demonstrated, whereas motor skills are more easily broken down into small linked parts that can be learnt gradually and it is obvious to the observer which stage has been reached.

A feature, perhaps of all Down's children, but it seems of Elizabeth at least, is that she needs to be very confident that she can 'get it right' before she will perform a skill. However, having once learnt it she will do it well. This was true of brick building: late in attainment, but then she put not only three bricks in a pile but five or six straight away.

The need to use the checklist flexibly ties up with the need for the home visitor and parents to act in close partnership. The parents are aware from day to day of the emerging skills and interests of their child and also of the needs of the family at this time. So skills can be learnt that fit in with the arrival of a new baby or the pregnancy of the mother, for example. If the parent provides an indication of the areas which need to be concentrated on, the home visitor has the skills to suggest specific activities to achieve these skills. (See Figures 5 and 6).

4. Dealing with boredom

As Elizabeth has grown more self-determined we have often had to find several ways to achieve an activity in one week to maintain her interest. Sometimes too it has been more successful if she has been unaware that we are 'doing Portage' and that it is important to me if she complies. A casual approach works best!

5. The achievement of checklist items

It has been difficult sometimes to decide when exactly Elizabeth has achieved a checklist item. This is sometimes due to ambiguity in the checklist but also to a refusal on Elizabeth's part to perform skills that she obviously possesses. The need to have a date by a checklist item has become less urgent as time has passed. We have begun to accept our little girl for the individual she is and are no longer obsessed with at what age she achieves this or that, as long as she

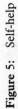

Figure 5: Self-help

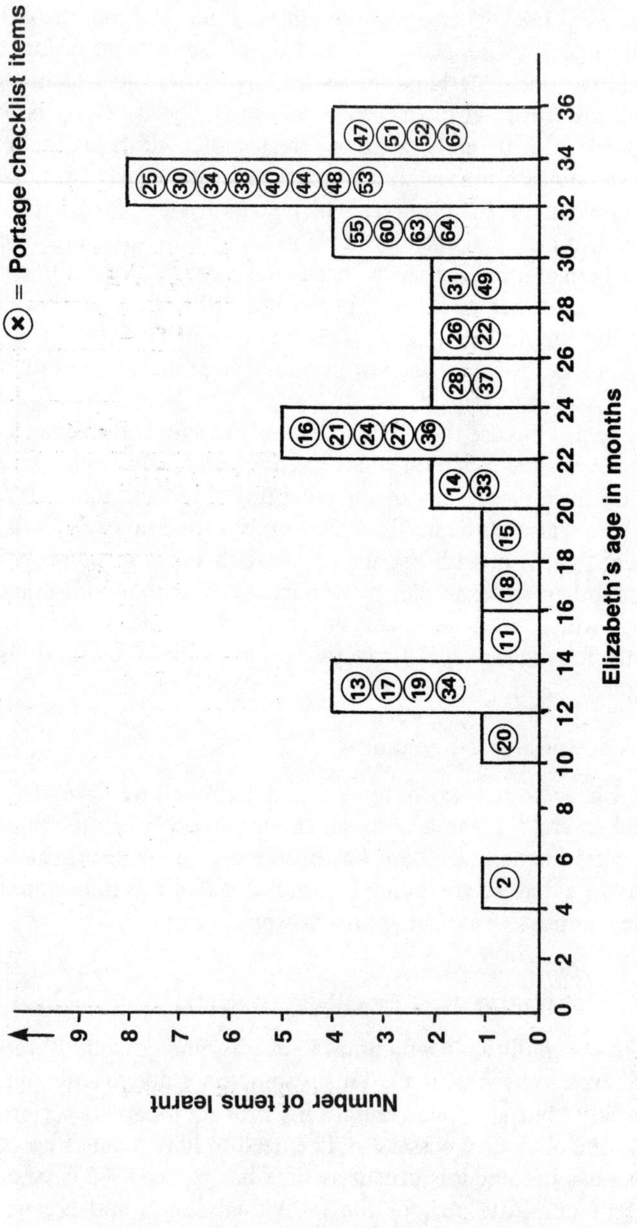

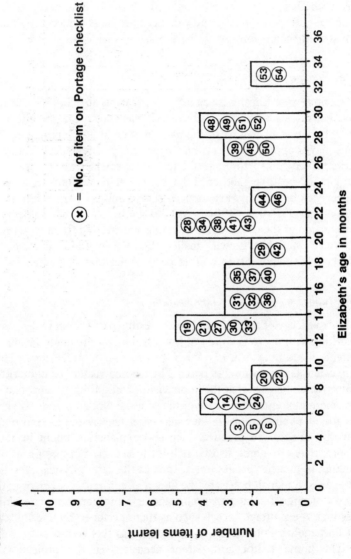

Figure 6: Socialization

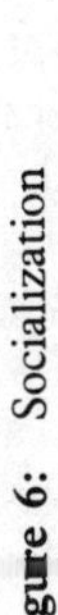

eventually acquires the skills she needs to fulfil her own individual potential and be equipped for her life.

In conclusion I would say that our approach to Portage and use of its methods has been closely tied in with the level of acceptance of our daughter's handicap, and this needs to be considered by home visitors in their approach to the family

Has Portage helped?

Definitely yes! Elizabeth has learnt a great number of skills. But it has helped me psychologically too. It has shown me ways to play with her and to be aware of the pattern of child development so that this play is appropriate. If it has helped me psychologically, it must have helped Elizabeth because I am perhaps in some ways a happier and more positive mother. I have written more fully in a small paperback book of my experiences in bringing up Elizabeth in these early years (Philps, 1984). As Elizabeth has grown older the proportion of the day spent in teaching specific skills in a structured 'Portage way' has grown smaller, but the methods involved in Portage have spun off into other parts of her play and activities.

The future: suggestions for improvement

My experience of the Portage Project results partly from two years of working with my own child but I was also lucky enough to be able to attend a training course which helped me a great deal. How important is the training of parents by a home visitor? Could written information be used that the home visitor could bring and explain on the methodology and practice of the project? Not all parents are able to attend a course, nor are they necessarily motivated to read much on this subject. So practical help and explanation might be most appropriate. It might also be helpful to see the Portage project as linking in to other programmes, such as the early physical exercises suggested for small babies by the Down's Children's Association, the Makaton Sign Language system, and/or a programme for teaching reading to encourage speech such as that developed by Sue Buckley at Portsmouth Polytechnic (a contributor to this volume).

The home visitor and parent need to see the project as a partnership with a two way flow of ideas and information. I was fortunate to find such a home visitor with whom a partnerhsip like this developed.

The home visitor's account

I work as a play therapist for the local health authority. This involves working with a small group of children who need specific help and who are mainly referred by doctors, health visitors and speech therapists. Three years ago I saw the Portage course advertised at work. On completion of the course I started to visit a child who is spastic. Six months later, when I had known Caroline for that time, Elizabeth, Caroline's first child, was born. She has Down's Syndrome. When she was five weeks old I made my initial Portage visit and a week later we were under way.

My expectations

Through my work I know the value of one-to-one contact with a child and how important it is to a child's development, expecially where there is a specific problem. I was excited at the prospect of working with Caroline and Elizabeth from the very beginning but also rather apprehensive. Although I am a mother myself the thought of dealing with a new-born baby made me feel a little lost. Apprehensive also, because with my own children I never recorded when and how they achieved any milestones in their development. I took them very much for granted. With Elizabeth I was to see things with completely different eyes. This association with Caroline was very much entered into as a partnership knowing full well that what we both wanted for Elizabeth would only be achieved by a mutual vision and pooling of ideas.

Our approach and how it has changed through time to adapt to Elizabeth's needs

On looking back the mistakes came to mind before the positive things, but I feel the mistakes were needed for us to go forward, for from these we learnt, and learnt together. The Infant Stimulation items on the checklist were very quickly achieved. Within four months we were through them all and very proud of ourselves. We had followed the list through and taken help from the cards; in fact we had followed everything to the letter, so much so that I can remember us both lying on the floor trying to decipher the instructions on how to roll a baby from back to front. The only surprise in that operation was that neither of us came out of it with dislocated arms.

As we branched out to greater things like 'Cognitive' and

'Socialization', life was suddenly not such plain sailing. Elizabeth developed likes and dislikes. She did not want to roll over when we wanted her to, she never wanted to push three blocks along train style and the thought of taking objects out of a container seemed to her just a waste of time.

Handling the checklist

How did we cope with those times? Well, it must be admitted that on some occasions we convinced ourselves that she had definitely achieved these goals just so we could escape them. In fact, there were many times that we decided that the checklist was written by idiots and that some of the goals were useless and unimportant and therefore a waste of time. But a week later we could usually face the problem realistically and sort something out.

It was then that we decided that we were not going to be slaves to a checklist order and that Elizabeth is an individual and we were going to treat her as such. That if she was going to achieve Motor 70 before Motor 20, which she did, then it was up to her and we were not going to restrict any progress through lack of vision. We found that by looking ahead on the checklist we could see skills emerging and those we encouraged. In this way we had successes and glaring failures. Sometimes, what we saw as emerging skills were almost figments of our imagination. Sometimes it took us a few weeks to realize it.

In one instance, Motor 10 was achieved in August 1981 and Motor 11 was not achieved until eight months later. With this and other areas where progress was slow it was hard not to feel too disheartened as we kept trying to think of new ideas, new ways to get Elizabeth motivated. At times it thoroughly drained us and our minds seemed to go blank.

Then finding the confidence to forget the checklist order and look ahead to see what new activity we could go on to gave us renewed incentive. I'm sure at those times Elizabeth breathed a sigh of relief. This was not to say we did not go back to the items missed out on the checklist. We did, and success eventually came.

Handling the activity charts

From times of despair as to how to encourage Elizabeth, we went to times of frustration when she could almost achieve a goal but then lose interest. It was then that we had to rack our brains over how to present that activity to her in a varied way. We found that she could lose interest in an activity in a matter of days, so to make out an activity chart specifically stating 'do this' and 'use that' was unsatisfactory. Therefore we had to think of alternatives so that she did not get bored. For example, in building a three-block tower we used various objects: tins, cotton reels, nesting toys as well as bricks. Though we were concentrating on the one activity the presentation had to be different every day. We found that whenever possible variety had to be our priority.

To help us in the times that we felt we were not progressing we devised our own recording system on the charts. This has taken many odd forms. To find out how best to encourage language, we recorded over many weeks all the different sounds that Elizabeth made and repeated them back to her. From this we could see some improvement and advance. On the other hand, when we dictated the sounds we wanted her to learn, we never seemed to get anywhere.

When we were trying to teach her to fetch an object from another room we varied the object we used. One 'object' was often daddy, so 'it' was recorded with a tick and a 'D' if successful. If the other object was a book, then a tick and a 'B' were recorded. We have found that this has made us more aware of the specific things that Elizabeth can do, and her preferences, and so has helped us to encourage her in the right directions. This has given us much-needed encouragement. It focuses on very small areas of achievement, but achievement nevertheless.

From the start two activities a week were chosen. Since Elizabeth was five months old four activities have been our usual weekly work, but more than that have been known! As Elizabeth has developed, her likes and dislikes have become very clear. What seemed to us good fun was to her a great bore, and after an initial show of interest, a day later she has not wanted to know. Having more activities has kept both Caroline and Elizabeth busy and happy. Also, having more than one activity to concentrate on has not pressurized Caroline into insisting that Elizabeth does this one thing because that is what she is supposed to be doing and it would feel like a week wasted if no progress were made.

When we first started out on Portage we had activities from most areas of the checklist every week. We found that in certain areas we would be ticking off goals as steady progress was made and that in other areas she seemed almost to be going backwards, not even doing what we knew she was capable of. It took a while for us to realize that she had spurts of learning in concentrated areas and that the way to handle these times was to encourage her in what she was ready for and not to get anxious because we were not moving forward in all areas. So from our dictating what we thought Elizabeth should be doing it has changed almost to letting her dictate to us. If she is going through a restless stage then there is no point in trying to insist that she sit down and do a puzzle. That does not mean to say that we do not forge ahead with long-term goals in mind and work towards them. We have found that we must be flexible in our thinking and in our attitudes.

Over the past two and a half years we have had our highs and lows. As the visitor going into the home I have often wanted to take with me the answers and solutions to our problems, but that is not how it is to be. We are a partnership working together and the trials and disappointments are to be shared along with the success and the joy, and that to me is what makes Portage work.

A review of parental involvement and the place of Portage

Sheila Wolfendale

Sheila Wolfendale is a Principal Lecturer with the Psychology Department of North East London Polytechnic.

Introduction

In this paper I hope to put parental involvement and partnership within a perspective of recent developments in education and the child-focused services, to see where Portage fits in within that context and what influence Portage itself may be having on attitudes to parenting and parental involvement, particularly for children with special educational needs.

If what we believe is that parents play a central and crucial role in their children's development and education, then it is my contention that we believe it because we now also believe that children are more important than they were in the past. The status of children has been raised immeasurably during the past hundred years.

We have evidence in writings and in pictures that children have in past times been maltreated, exploited and abandoned. Attitudes have been reflected in accounts, folklore, medical treatises.

Some examples

1. The early Anglo-Saxons carried out tests to discover whether an infant had the courage necessary to face the hardships of life. He was placed on a sloping roof or the bough of a tree. If he laughed he was taken down and reared, whereas signs of fear and crying meant death.

2. In the seventh century an ecclesiastic law stated 'If a woman place her infant by the hearth and a man put water in the cauldron and it boil over and the child be scalded to death,

the woman must do penance for her negligence.' Neglect was common.

3. A medieval writer warns: 'Fondness and familiarity breed contempt and irreverency in children.'

4. In Puritan times there was a series of little books warning children not to rely on God's mercy for any 'sins' – 'Children who lye, play the truant and break the Sabbath will go into everlasting burning.' Parental assistance in keeping their children away from these eternal terrors was to make them learn catechism and scripture excerpts by heart.

5. Public punishments continued to be severe into the nineteenth century. Infant pickpockets went to prison; one is reputed to have cried for his mother on the scaffold; in 1813 two boys of ten and 12 years were sentenced to seven years' transportation for stealing warehouse linen.

The massive social and educational advances of the reforming nineteenth and twentieth centuries betokened changing private and public attitudes to children. The extermination of much disease meant that more children survived, thus life itself was more precious and the increasing liberation for many parents from the gruelling tyranny of a 12–hour working day for minimal amounts of recompense meant, over time, that parents have been able to act as caregivers to their own children. Contemporary attitudes are that children have a central, not an incidental or peripheral place in their parents' lives, even when parents have a commitment to their own continuing personal development.

The perspective of former events and past attitudes makes clearer why there is much public and official belief at present that parents have a unique contribution to make to their own children's development and education. In addition to their basic duties to feed, clothe and house them, parents also support and nurture their children.

What is now recognized is not that parents are being 're-discovered' as playing such a prime part, but that all of us (parents, professional carers, public persons) realize that these age-old duties provide the best springboard from which to develop and carry out other activities that will positively promote and enhance children's development and education.

What is parenting?

The list presented below summarizes most of the functions of being a parent. These are carried out all the time parents and parent-figures have the responsibility for children. Some we are aware of – they are obvious and tangible: making meals, keeping clothes clean, etc. Others we think of less in a conscious sense, for they are more pervasive and possibly more abstract. The list of 1–11 is intended to denote the range as well as the depth of parental involvement in children's development and early and continuing education. Of course there are individual differences in emphasis as well as style.

Parenting functions are:

1. to provide means of survival ('primary' needs)
2. to provide emotional support and endorsement ('secondary' needs)
3. to provide the setting for emotional development to occur
4. to provide an environment in which exploration and hypothesis testing can take place
5. to provide the frame of reference against and in which exploration *outside* the home can take place
6. to provide a protective environment
7. to provide opportunities and direction for the growth of independent functioning and self-organization
8. to act as models (language, emotional/social behaviour)
9. to train and guide the young towards understanding of and adherence to social norms (controls and restraints)
10. to act as possessors and transmitters of knowledge and information about the world
11. to act as decision-makers and arbiters of decisions, minute by minute and in longer term.

Not only are there individual differences of emphasis and style, but parents can and do vary and modify these functions. Child-rearing is a dialogue and a communication between parents and child, and irrespective of whether or not a child is a quick or slow learner, or a child with 'special needs', an interactive rhythm between parent and child is set up from very early on.

Some of these functions, perhaps all, translate into or become *parenting skills*. Some of us can become expert in routines with our children, perhaps very knowledgeable. One of the basic premises that underlies parent-professional partnership ventures *is* that parents have well-developed skills; this theme will permeate my paper.

It is part of parenthood to have aspirations for children, whether or not these are modest or ambitious. Ask yourselves, those of you who are parents, what yours are or have been. If we all shared our thoughts on what we have wanted or do want for our children, we would find that there would be some common aspirations and some others unique to our own situations.

I should like at this point to say that I feel that it is high time that parental and public aspirations for children's education and welfare were voiced and shared. I contend that parents' own views on their approaches to child rearing, to child management, what they want from education and what they hope for their children have largely gone unexplored and unrecorded except for isolated pieces of research, such as the longitudinal study of the Newsons at Nottingham University. As a result, at times, officialdom in the form of professionals and administrators has made recommendations which it believes are in the best interests of the child, only to find that they have not accorded with the parents' wishes, let alone the parents' or guardians' perceptions and understanding of the situation. One example might be a recommendation for residential education, or transfer to another school. Removal into care is of course yet another example, where case notes can provide eloquent testimony of many a mismatch between public and private aspirations.

Observations so far have been a preamble building up to a central point, and one intimately connected with the theme of the book *Parental Involvement in Primary Schoiols* (Cyster *et al.*, 1979). If we are to accept 'the importance of parents' as a philosophy it has to be translated into action that affects and pervades every facet of parent-professional contact that purports to be on behalf of children. This is the wider context into which Portage fits and is one which I wish to explore through consideration of recent contributions in the area of parental involvement in children's development and education. I will give a brief overview of:

- government reports
- mainstream parental involvement

- community-parent-school cooperation
- parental involvement in reading
- developments in special educational needs and parental involvement.

Government reports and the place of parents

Each of the reports of education and child services from Plowden to Warnock has drawn attention to and emphazised the potential of collaboration between professionals and parents to enhance children's development and learning. Thus the Plowden Report (1967) asserts 'By involving the parents, the children may be helped' (para. 114). The Bullock Report (1975) on the teaching of English and reading commended school initiatives of the early 1970's which aimed to involve parents, usually mothers, in early reading and language activities, and endorsed the growing idea at that time of the home liaison teacher. The Court Committee (Court Report, 1976) felt that 'families could be better at bringing up their children if they were given the right information, support and relationships with the caring professions when it was needed and in a more acceptable way' (p. 25). The Taylor Report (1977) called for increased numbers of parents as school governors, a recommendation which was subsequently incorporated into the 1980 Education Act. Finally the Warnock Report (1978) included a chapter entitled 'Parents as Partners' and called for improved working relationships between school and home, professionals and parents. Incidentally, Chapter 5 of the Warnock Report contains a description of the Portage Project drawing on that example and the existing provision for peripatetic teachers of the young child with hearing impairment. The Warnock Committee went on strongly to recommend a 'comprehensive peripatetic teaching service which would cater, wherever possible, exclusively for children with disabilities or significant difficulties below school age' (p. 83). One of its central briefs would be to work with and provide support for parents.

Parental involvement in education

There is a common consensus that there was virtually no parent-school contact prior to the 1960s and in many a school one saw a notice 'no parents beyond this point'. Since the Plowden Report there have been several surveys which confirm that over the last fifteen years there has been a trend towards greater parental presence in schools. Surveys in 1972 reported modest increases in numbers of parents coming into school, to help with cooking, painting, hearing children read; a survey by the National Foundation for Educational Research (Cyster *et al.*, 1979) into parental involvement in primary schools reported an expansion of these activities. I have summarized this trend below.

Table 1: Parents and schools: continuum of contact and involvement

no contact	minimal contact	moderate contact	moderate involvement	considerable involvement	partner-ship
	Open evenings, concerts, plays, written reports	PTA	Parent hears reading, helps with painting, cooking, Newsletters	Home reading/ parents' room, home liaison, parent-teacher workshops, community base	

Parents' rights and representations in education

Some of the Taylor Report's recommendations became enshrined in the 1980 Education Act and have extended parents' rights and access to the educational process, certainly in principle and to some extent in reality. Thus in the act we find:
Section 2: all state schools to have parents and teachers as elected representatives on the governing body
Section 6: parents have a right to express a preference for the school they wish their child to attend and to state reasons
Section 8: Local Education Authorities are compelled to publish information regarding schools (rules governing admission, etc.)

Parents, school and the community

Quite a number of home-school collaborative projects were set up within the EPA (Educational Priority Area) programme, or, later, urban-aid funded programme. Some of these were ambitious, research-oriented projects, others were low-key, modest local ventures. All attempted to demonstrate in practice these principles:

- parental involvement in the learning process helps the child
- parents have a positive contribution to make to development and education

- some of parents' needs can be met through these means
- schools and teachers benefit from closer liaison.

Best known examples of current initiatives include Coventry Community Education, Liverpool Parent Support Programme, Milton Keynes Home Link and Newham Parent's Centre.

Parental involvement in reading

This is a rapidly burgeoning area, and its recent and current history includes several well-known projects (Belfield, Haringey, Derbyshire, Hackney) as well as a considerable number of localized and unpublicized ventures, which may be short-term projects or routinely form part of a school's provision.

By now there is beginning to be quite a literature on the subject of home and school-based parental involvement in reading programmes, in which teachers and parents work towards agreed objectives, using pre-prepared materials (school books, library loans, work sheets and so on). It is possible to pinpoint the main characteristics, elements and considerations involved in developing a 'technology' of parental involvement in reading. Some of these are:

Roles: what parts will the teacher, parent and child agree to play and what will be the areas of responsibility?
Who for: will the programme be aimed at initial learners (infant school children) developing reading skills, or children with reading difficulties?
Material: school books; library loan; remedial/resource centre loan; pre-prepared cards and sheets
Type of programme: paired reading; child reading; parent reading; language-based approach. What kind of correction and reinforcement will be built in?
Training: for teacher(s) and parents. Meetings, visits, use of video. How many sessions?
Measurement and Recording: selection criteria: samples; controls and comparisons; pre and post assessment measures; monitoring and probing; record keeping; when and where to see parents
Time-span: decide at planning stage length of the reading programme; build in renewable options
Criteria for evaluation: results of pre and post and any other assessment; teachers', parents', children's, others' views; follow-up; cost effectiveness criteria; repeatability and generalizability.

Many current programmes are incorporating some or all of these elements.

Parents and special educational needs

Many Portage workers will be familiar with and expert in some areas where progress has been rapid in the last few years, where parents have become involved in assessment and diagnosis, where parents have become involved in teaching their children and assisting their development, and where parents have become involved in decision-making. A brief summary of some of this work is presented below. For more detail, see Wolfendale 1983, Chapter 7.

Table 2: Parents and special educational needs

INVOLVEMENT IN	EXAMPLES AND REFERENCES
Assessment Diagnosis	Hester Adrian Research Centre (Mittler and McConachie 1983) Child Development Research Unit, Nottingham University (Newson and Hipgrave 1982) Portage (Cameron 1982)
Teaching own child and Assisting development	Portage Yule and Carr (1980)
Behaviour Problems	Westmacott and Cameron (1981) Newson and Hipgrave
Group support Workshops Home visits	Southend (in Pugh 1981) Hester Adrian Research Centre Honeylands (in Pugh 1981)

This work is based on the following premises:

- that parents are experts on their own children
- that their skills complement professional skills
- that parents can impart vital information and make informed observations
- that parents have the right to be involved

- that parents should contribute to decision-making and
- that parents can be highly effective teachers of their own children.

1981 Education Act

This Act amends the law relating to special education, and came into force on 1st April 1983. Some have said that it is a blueprint for partnership with parents; others say that not much will change in regard to parent-professional relationships and parental say in allocation to special or mainstream schools. Under the Act, parents' rights are extended in respect of processes of pre-referral discussion with schools, psychologists and others, referral for assessment, opportunities to present *their* views, to be involved in discussion over placement, the best provision for meeting special educational needs, and review processes. Parents have the right to appeal to local Appeal Committees, or to the Secretary of State. Thus the legal framework for parental participation in these processes is now in existence. Time will tell whether or not parents and workers in the child services will work together more closely to become partners in the enterprise.

I have attempted to provide a brief review of recent developments in parental involvement in various aspects of their children's development and educational experience. It is clear that parents are being acknowledged as *contributors* to children's development and education. Nowadays they are regarded far less as clients with the client characteristics of being dependent on experts' opinions, passive in the receipt of services, apparently in need of redirection, peripheral to decision-making and perceived as 'inadequate,' and 'deficient'.

Whether or not parents are regarded as partners in all these areas of involvement is rather more open to debate if we accept that major characteristics of parents as partners would include their being active and central in decision-making and its implementation, having equal strengths and equivalent expertise, able to contribute to as well as receive services, and that because they share responsibility, they and professionals are mutually accountable.

There are as yet few examples of parent-professional partnership. However, Portage is one.

The place of Portage

As is now well known, Portage originated in Portage, Wisconsin, USA, and took its title from its place of origin. What may be less well known but of significance is what the word 'portage' means. The dictionaries define it thus:

> 'carrying' (French *porter,* to carry); 'carrying of boats or goods between two navigable waters, place, at which this is necessary'; 'act of carrying'.

The symbolic point I want to make is that the Portage project is demonstrating just this quality of carrying. It is spreading all over the country. It involves whole networks of parents and different professionals and other workers who have never worked together before. It is spreading into schools and being seen as appropriate for various age-groups. Its philosophy is pervasive and influential; the ideas being demonstrated and 'proved' in practice are that

- parents are effective assessors of their own children
- parents can become skilled teachers of their children
- parents are equally involved with decision-making.

It would be, perhaps, timely to remind ourselves of some basic historic facts concerning Portage.

(i) It was funded in 1969 under the Education of the Handicapped Act, Public Law 91-230, Title 6, Part C, which sought to 'develop, implement and demonstrate a model program serving young handicapped children in rural areas' (i.e., Portage, Wisconsin).

(ii) It initially served 23 school districts in South Central rural Wisconsin.

(iii) By 1972 the Portage model had been selected nationally as one of eight exemplary pre-school programs for the handicapped.

(iv) By 1975 the Joint Dissemination Review Panel of the US Office of Education unanimously validated the total Portage model for national dissemination and replication.

(v) In the early 1970s it was spreading to different parts of the USA, particularly Iowa, Missisippi, Georgia, North Dakota, Texas, Arizona and Arkansas, and by 1977 it was being replicated and carried out in over 30 'sites' in the USA (over 60 services were reported).

(vi) In the United Kingdom during 1977 the Wessex Portage Project issued its report, and later in the year the Portage Service in South Glamorgan also reported.

(vii) In 1978 the Warnock Report described and commended the Portage Service.

The rest, as they say, is history... Portage now belongs to the present and to the future.

I want to round off my paper by suggesting that, as parents become increasingly involved in many facets of children's development and education, the skills and expertise developed by parents who are involved with Portage have relevance beyond the Portage programme. The influence of parents via and through Portage is potentially immense for involvement in assessment, report-writing, contributing to statements, deciding on placement and reviewing special educational provision. Involvement in Portage for parents can lead to increased knowledge of child development, of the ways in which children acquire skills, of methods of teaching and conveying teaching points, of ways of supporting children, existing child services and provision and the procedures of the 1981 Education Act. These experiences will, it is hoped, promote the ability to support and sustain other parents and act as catalysts in bringing professionals closer together.

Learning Language Skills

Generalizing Early Language Skills: a programme of activities designed to stimulate the acquisition of words for common objects

Mollie White

Mollie White worked as a senior home teacher with the Winchester Health Authority's Portage service. She now lectures at King Alfred's College, Winchester.

This paper describes a programme of activities carried out during the course of one year with Jacob, a Down's Syndrome boy who was one year old at the outset of the programme. When the year began Jacob was not discriminating any specific object word. During the course of the year he acquired skills which showed comprehension of the names of most common objects together with picture symbols of those objects and demonstrated these skills in a wide variety of settings.

The programme analyses the *breakdown of the teaching objectives* leading to Jacob's long-term response, the *timing* of those objectives, and the use of *presentation* to maintain and generalize each acquired skill. It gives particular attention to the difficulties of maintaining interest in the programme during the early stages when Jacob's progress was relatively slow.

Many of the problems concerned with teaching and generalizing early language skills are concerned with the apparent slow rate of the child's progress. As each new skill is acquired and generalized into the child's repertoire there needs to be much practice of that skill in a wide variety of settings over a long period of time. The time factor produces problems for parents and teachers. There are difficulties in maintaining interest in a specific skill over a long period and the temptation to abandon teaching activities which focus on generalizing a familiar skill and turn to activities which explore exciting *new* skills is very great. Moreover, an unrealistic forecast of the number of activities necessary to the generalization of a given skill can result in a sense of failure when the programme continues much longer than anticipated.

The following example illustrates the nature of the problem. The first time the child responds to the word 'teddy' by turning towards his own teddy sitting as always in the corner of his cot is very exciting. Everyone around the child is delighted. Finding the same teddy in another setting is less dramatic. By the time the child is recognizing all teddies, not merely his own, in response to the word 'teddy', that first response will have become a dim memory. Yet all these responses are necessary to the child's comprehension of 'teddy'. If we add to this history a parallel one which begins with the child being guided by his mother to look at a picture of a teddy carefully placed beside his own teddy, and ends with the same child able to pick out a simple image of any teddy in any book, then we are considering a long and complex process all concerned with word and picture symbols for one object, teddy. It is hardly surprising that with so many materials, occasions and settings to consider teachers and parents give up careful monitoring of the process and leave much of it to chance.

Is chance good enough? Does the Portage teaching model, as the critics of direct instruction suggest, fail to develop in children 'a genuine understanding of the objects and events in their world' (McConkey 1981)? Or can we improve on chance by building 'generalisation and adaptation into our teaching programmes' (Cameron, 1982)? Is there a pattern to the child's increasing comprehension that we can shape through the use of appropriate activities? Can we at the same time maintain the child's and our own interest in a lengthy teaching programme?

The following programme of activities looks at these questions. It was designed to stimulate Jacob's comprehension of the names of common objects, leading to his later expression of object words. The programme was carried out by Jacob's family during the course of one year. It is presented in five parts. The first part, A, refers to Jacob's skill level at the outset of the programme. It is important to emphasize that the skills described here were vital to the design of the programme that follows. The other four parts B, C, D, and E represent four clear stages in the development of Jacob's comprehension of a wide number of words and picture symbols for common objects.

The text refers to behaviours from the portage Checklist and the Wessex Revised Portage Language Checklist.*

A The background of acquired skills

Listening and attending (Level One)

Jacob had acquired high level listening and attending skills. He continually sought eye contact with any adult, particularly members of his family. Their attention brought ready smiles and vocalizations. Jacob was alert to a wide variety of domestic sounds, musical sounds, and the sound of voices, in particular his own name, from across a room to which he responded in anticipation of attention.

Early vocalizations (Level One)

Jacob responded with vocalizations to a wide variety of sound stimuli but he showed a marked preference for a human voice. He responded to his parents' voices with smiles, coos, and babbling, taking part in 'pretend' conversations.

Imitation (Level One)

Jacob was beginning to imitate simple gestures such as clapping hands. He watched with interest gestures that accompanied songs and rhymes and moved his hands and arms in response. Precise imitation was guided by his parents in simple turn-taking games.

Responding to objects

Jacob had learnt to focus on, reach out, and grasp objects. He *discriminated favourite objects, giving them a prolonged response*. He did not associate words with these objects. Games using small objects

---

*The Wessex Revised Portage Language Checklist has extended the language section of the Portage Guide to Early Education Checklist to provide

i) an enlarged developmental sequence of language behaviours
ii) a grouping of those behaviours under major language skill headings
iii) a set of activity cards to accompany new behaviours in the sequence
iv) a set of adult behaviours in relation to each stage of the child's development; 4 stages covering development between birth and four years.

and containers were in regular use. Many of Jacob's motor activities (reaching from a sitting position, moving into a crawling position, kneeling etc.) were rewarded with favourite objects.

Time scale: One year preceding the programme that follows.

B Stage one: achieving a listening response to a small vocabulary of eight object words

Choosing and preparing the objects

Jacob's parents chose a number of objects that aroused a prolonged looking and handling response from Jacob. These were:

a doll	a 'Pooh' bear on a stick
a rattle	a ball
a cup	a boat and two little men
a spoon	a car

The names of these objects which were already in regular use were to be the starting point for Jacob's listening response to object words. At the same time a set of pictures was selected (here they were drawn and coloured by Jacob's mother) to match the objects.

Presentation

Because these objects were already in frequent use, it was decided that to focus Jacob's attention on the object names during existing routines would be unlikely to achieve success. Too many competing stimuli were present. The following behaviours were chosen as appropriate first targets:

> Jacob will watch mother and give eye contact to a named object. (See Example C in introduction to Wessex Revised Language Checklist.)
>
> Jacob will be guided to touch the picture with the matching object. (The picture was a new stimulus. While Jacob was guided through the touching procedure the picture and object were named clearly.)

These activities were continued and objects introduced one by one until all the listed objects were in use.

Time scale: three months.

C Stage two: the use of games to transfer the presentation of eight object names into a variety of settings

An *attentive, listening response* to the names of eight specific objects having been established, this response was maintained and linked to other settings.

The two objectives were:

(i) to maintain frequent repetition of the object names and Jacob's response to them, and
(ii) to stimulate Jacob's association of these names with a variety of activities.

These objectives were achieved through a play approach.

Children's games

There is a considerable literature devoted to the function of children's games. Practising newly acquired skills is the function that concerns us here and it is worth noting that during the period immediately following the acquisition of any new skill the practice of that skill provides strong reinforcement to the child. The pleasure that the child derives from the game ensures its frequent repetition (Millar, 1968). We selected games which allowed Jacob to practise recently acquired skills from all areas of his development and built into these games his ongoing experience of the eight object words. The following games show the links with other areas of the checklist.

Jacob responded to 'peep-bo' games with listed objects (L27*, Soc 18)

Jacob waved 'bye bye' to listed objects as they were put away (L29, Soc 20)

Jacob found the 'hidden' named object (Cog 10)

---

*L + number refers to Wessex Revised Checklist numbers
Soc/Cog + number refers to original Portage checklist numbers

L = Language Soc = Socialization Mot = Motor SH = Self-Help Cog = Cognitive

Jacob picked out a named object (no choices) from a container to a 'Where's...?' cue (L39 Cog 10)

Jacob used a named object appropriately when given help, e.g., pushed car, rolled ball, ate with spoon, drank from cup: these activities were presented as turn-taking routines (L30, L54)

Jacob was guided to mime action songs using named objects, (L48) e.g. 'This is the way we roll the ball,' and so on

Jacob looked at pictures for a few seconds (L43). This was sometimes followed by looking for matching object

Jacob went on 'Object Walks' – 'Let's find the...' with help (Mot)

Time scale: three months.

During this three-month period Jacob learnt to clap and wave 'bye-bye' independently. A rattling from inside a container led him to investigate the contents. Certain imitation games, e.g. rolling a ball, pushing a car, achieved an independent response. He was *beginning* to look spontaneously towards the listed objects when they were named but this response was not 100 per cent.

D Stage three: achieving an independent ('looking towards' or 'handling') named objects and picture; adding new vocabulary

Throughout the previous stage Jacob was becoming increasingly familiar with a small vocabulary of object names in a number of contexts. An independent response of 'looking towards' or 'handling' the named object was beginning to emerge. Stage Three reinforces this independent response. Sample behaviours were as follows:

Jacob would look at/touch/pick up named objects in response to

'Where's...? (L*58)

Objects were presented in clear space but with other objects present

The request was made before all routines which involved the objects. Success would be followed with an appropriate play routine

Jacob would touch (point to) a named picture, given a choice of two (L59)

Jacob would imitate gestures independently, using named objects in turn-taking games and songs (L30)

Adding new vocabulary

Stage Three also sees the introduction of new vocabulary. Vocabulary was selected according to 'Early Speech Behaviours: Words for Objects' in the Revised Wessex Language Checklist:

clothes (hat, socks, shoes, coat)
toys (bird, bricks, book)
animals (dog, cat, cow, lamb, duck)
food (drink, biscuit, orange, banana, cake)
family names (mama, dada, Sue, baby)
parts of the body (hair, arm, hand, toes, eyes, knees).

Matching pictures were also used where possible.

These objects names were introduced in the structured settings described under Stage One. Jacob's accelerated response meant that new groups of words could be introduced every few weeks. Following their initial introductory period, these object words also became part of Jacob's play.

Time scale: six months ongoing

E Stage four: the outcome – Jacob responds to words for common objects and to pictures of those objects spontaneously

Jacob's response to a vocabulary which included the original eight objects and those introduced in Stage Three was well established at the end of the year. He would 'fetch' and 'give' those objects on request. He would point to them in picture books. He was however still associating specific objects with their names. Stage Four generalizes these object words to include the class of objects described, e.g. cups, spoons. Typical objectives included:

Jacob will collect all his . . . (cars)

Jacob and his family will collect sets of . . . (toys, animals)

Jacob will find named object in different picture books (e.g. cat in a number of books)

Jacob will point to a number of examples of the same object

As this stage was established Jacob responded to picture symbols in entirely new material when asked 'Where's the...?' He was also beginning to discriminate between particular objects which were similar, e.g. Jacob's sock and Sue's sock. Practice with actions and objects was continuing during his play routines and the naming of action pictures was introduced into his picture book games. Background skills for teaching later language skills in Level Three, particularly the use of action words and two-word strings, thus became a natural outcome of generalizing acquired skills.

Expressive language

Although the focus of this account has been the acquisition of a response to object words rather than the expression of those words, clearly their expression was the long-term aim. Expression follows comprehension and the time factor varies from child to child. By the time Stage Four was in progress Jacob was using spontaneously ten words and four animal noises. He was also imitating others when they were repeated back to him during play routines. (See Behaviours listed under Level Two – Early Speech (Wessex).)

Conclusion

The relatively small steps taken by Jacob during the early stages of the programme compared to his accelerated response later emphasizes the importance of the flexibility of the Portage teaching model. The design of individual teaching activities which responded to the child's ongoing strengths and needs allows for variation of the necessary practice of small step skills to be built into the programme. Selecting play activities that are reinforcing for both parent and child ensures the necessary repetition. Teaching strategies which examine all areas of the child's development as the basis for the design of appropriate play generate the 'natural' transfer of acquired skills. Jacob's ability to acquire new vocabulary later in the programme, and his spontaneous use of that vocabulary in unfamiliar settings and in response to new materials, suggests that teaching programmes based on the Portage model which utilize such strategies *are* capable of stimulating the generalization and adaptation of learnt skills.

The First Words and First Sentences Language Programme

Bill Gillham

Bill Gillham directs the M.Sc. course in Educational Psychology at the University of Strathclyde.

The *First Words Language Programme* had its origins in an interest in the relationship between language *comprehension* and language *production* at the first words stage. At the common-sense level it seemed clear that young children (and language retarded children) understood a large number of words before they produced words to express their own interests, intentions, and so on. From this it followed that a possible way in to developing purposeful speech in children with few words (or even no words) would be to focus on developing their understanding of the meaning of a vocabulary that might be useful to them.

It was assumed from the beginning that a focus on 'getting the child to say the word' is based on a misconception of what independent language is about. A programme that does not lead to spontaneous language use – the child producing words when *he or she* wants to for *his or her* purposes – is no language programme at all. However, that was one of the few things that we *did* get right at the beginning.

Early trials

Our early work centred on developing techniques for teaching word comprehension in short 'focus' sessions of 10–20 minutes. At a practical level this went quite well – the children showed improved comprehension; what they didn't show was much improvement in production. It was some time before we realized that it was necessary to distinguish between comprehension-adequate-for-comprehension and comprehension-adequate-for-production. The first is a *recognition* process – the word is presented (spoken) and the child has to recognize it; the second is a *recall* process – a situation arises where the necessary word has to be recollected without any external help. Clearly recall is more difficult: the implications for comprehension training are that it has to be so organized that the vocabulary that is taught goes in and stays there, available for recall when needed. This insight was an important discovery and what we did in consequence was to devise three levels of comprehension training:

- simple demonstration
- choice discrimination tasks
- interactive doll play with the vocabulary items brought in as part of a simple story.

Following the development of this procedure, there was an improvement in the spontaneous use of the words being taught by the children we were working with. But results were still not impressive: something was evidently wrong. It is embarrassing to have to recall what it was.

One thing that never occurred to us initially as a particular problem was deciding what words to teach: it seemed obvious – common objects, colours, numbers, simple verbs, prepositions and the like. The only thing that can be said in our defence was that it didn't seem to be a serious problem to anyone else either. But then a student, James Thatcher, drew attention to a monograph by Katherine Nelson of Yale University (Nelson, 1973). As part of a larger study she had asked the mothers of 19 babies to keep written records of their first 50 words. Nelson analysed the total vocabulary in various ways: her results were something of a revelation. Apparently many of the words we had tried to teach were not used by children at the one word stage. Many common objects were not referred to at all: notably absent were the numbers and colours on which we had expended so much effort. The lesson was obvious: if the children were not producing the words we were teaching perhaps it was because we were not teaching them words they wanted to produce.

We replicated the study on a sample of 14 Nottingham babies, but asking the mothers to keep records for the first hundred words. Our results closely matched the American data on high frequency words. But did 'normal' data apply to the mentally handicapped? I followed up four Down's children (not in our remediation study) for their first fifty words: they talked about the same kinds of things as other children (see Gillham, 1981).

Our teaching objectives were radically revised in the light of this research, with very satisfactory results. Gillham (1981) reports evaluation data on six children; McGlynn (1980) reports on three others.

The evaluation

The actual working of the programme is described in Gillham (1979) and need not be repeated here. But a brief account of the evaluation technique is in order. Conventionally, if you want to evaluate a programme you employ one group who get the 'treatment' – the experimental group, and one group who do not (or get some placebo treatment) – the control group. Each group has to consist of matched individuals. Matching human beings has always been a dubious exercise; it becomes almost impossible where mentally handicapped children are concerned. That is one problem. The other problem is a social one. People (parents, teachers, nurses) who care for the handicapped do not like to feel that one group is being 'deprived' whilst the other is receiving special treatment: what they do as a result of this can confound the 'experimental' method. For these reasons a 'single-case' experimental design was adopted in evaluating the First Words programme. Instead of an experimental and control group of children, we had experimental and control groups of words. Pairs of words of the same form-class and the same level of frequency in our data were selected from those words the child had not yet produced. From each pair one word was randomly assigned to an experimental (goal) group and the other to a control group. Parents maintained records of *all* new words produced. If 'goal' words appeared significantly more often than 'control' words in spontaneous use then the programme was having an effect; if not then it wasn't. This was the technique employed in evaluating the programme. It is also a technique which can be used by practitioners in judging the usefulness of the programme with a particular child.

Influences on further research

When I was working on the First Words Language Programme project, two of the mothers who were being helped to teach single words to their Down's syndrome children independently reported that the children were showing signs of reading word cards that they had stuck up on the wall. I had asked the mothers to put up these cards as reminders for themselves as to the words they were currently teaching. Most of them were attached to pictures and the mothers would point to the picture, name it, and talk about it. However, both of them came to believe that their children were reading the words rather than naming the pictures. I asked them to check on this by making use of flash cards only, which they did, and I observed the process myself. At the time the children (both boys) were able to do this they had a mental age of approximately two to two and half years (slightly over half their chronological age) and had around fifty single words in their spoken vocabulary. Both of the mothers felt their learning to read the words helped the children to remember the words for use in speech. The surprising thing was that these two mentally handicapped children appeared to learn the words easily in this fashion – much more easily than they learnt many other things their mothers have tried to teach them. It was almost as if they had an aptitude for it.

But was it anything more than a curio? Could it be exploited in any way? If a child is mentally handicapped then his or her special abilities should surely be used to his or her advantage. But how?

At about this time we were addressing ourselves to the task of constructing a First Sentences programme. The First Words Programme was going well and it was clear that in most cases it effectively promoted an increase in vocabulary. But many of the children who were making gains in that direction were showing no signs of putting words together. I remember asking one of the mothers we were working with what she thought the problem was. She remarked 'It seems as if he can't hold on to one word and then find the other one in his memory. He knows both the words, but he can't find them together.' That suggested a problem of *retrieval*.

At the same time we were coming to grips with the theoretical problem of whether children were using grammatical rules from the time they started to combine words (it seemed fairly clear that they weren't), and, if that were the case, where the 'rule idea' came from. The American psycholinguist Martin Braine, in his 1976 monograph 'Children's first word combinations' suggests that first combinations are not rule-governed, but are assembled to meet particular semantic needs, and therefore rather idiosyncratically. From such assemblages the child may perceive that a rule could be said to operate within that combination and, on the basis of that cognitive discovery, construct other word combinations of the same type (or according to the same rule). The alternative explanation, very simply, is that the child is born 'programmed' to construct sentences (the idea of a language acquisition device) so that he or she derives grammar from adult utterances, a puzzling achievement since the child's first sentences are often substantially different from anything adults produce (at least, under normal conditions).

If Martin Braine is right (and his proposal seems eminently reasonable) then the problem for the practitioner concerned to help a child stuck at the one-word stage is how to help him or her to recall words in combination whilst appreciating the separateness of the words. Only if this is appreciated will the child be able to perceive a rule operating between those words.

It is quite a simple matter to teach a one-word-stage child to produce two-word phrases, but these tend to be treated as if they were one word – there is no progress beyond that point. They may be used appropriately, but just operate as 'set phrases'.

Reading, language development and first sentences

My experience of the two Down's children learning to read words led me to explore the possibility of developing word recognition skills in mentally handicapped and language retarded children at the one-word stage as a means of enabling them to recall the separate elements of a 'sentence' and appreciating that those elements were separate (and so could be recombined in different ways).

We tend to think of an understanding of written words as being an 'advanced' stage of a child's development. But our discoveries show that this is not necessarily so. It is also to see that 'visual' words have some important advantages over 'heard' words. For example:

- they stand still: you can inspect them for as long as you like;
- they are physically separate and can easily be seen as distinct from each other;
- they bring in visual memory to support auditory memory of particular words;
- it is easy to demonstrate the separation and recombination of written words.

The materials

Using these ideas we went on to devise a set of book materials (essentially sets of six to ten cards clipped together) centred on regular and routine topics in a child's day which we judged to have language/communication potential, e.g. bathtime, going to the lavatory (very popular), daddy coming home, and so on.

Initially we used sets of photographs but these were surprisingly unsuccessful and we now use black-and-white cartoon-type illustrations, each linked with a two-element sentence of the kind which has high-frequency use in normal child language (as evidenced by our analysis of mothers' written records of the first 50 sentences produced by a sample of 15 children). All the sentences are of the kind which have generative rule potential and the intention is that the child first learns to 'read' at least some of the depictable words separately on cards, and then proceeds to the books with the parent or teacher weaving a 'personal' story round the series of pictures/sentences and the child saying his or her sentence at the appropriate points. In this way the child learns not just to say the sentence, but also how to use it meaningfully in a story that parallels real-life usage.

Our materials are designed to have wide application and they have proved acceptable to a range of children. The illustrations can be coloured and 'personalized' in various ways (hair coloured, glasses added, and so on). Even the unisex child can be made more 'masculine' or 'feminine' if desired. Most interesting has been the ease and willingness with which mentally handicapped children have identified with the characters in the line drawings: there are exceptions to this but in general this has occurred without hesitation.

With the book materials there is a controlled repetition of sentence types so that the child experiences more than one example of each sentence, which nudges him or her in the direction of rule perception. The hoped-for progression is:

- transferring the actual sentences in the books to the parallel real-life situations (which often occurs very quickly);
- the generation of original sentences of the same type (i.e. saying 'Peter come', having learnt to say 'Daddy come').

It has been difficult to evaluate these processes using a single-case design but results are encouraging, being mainly related to the extent that individual children learn to 'read' words. Those who do (mostly usually Down's children) appear to have a clear advantage in learning, productively, word combinations; some children can learn all the depictable words; a few can recognize no words in this way. In any case we take them on to the book materials since this also acts as a check on our original assumptions.

The manual and card materials have now been published (by Allen and Unwin and Learning Development Aids respectively). Our book-card materials have been carefully designed and suit most needs. But they are not indispensable and it is perfectly possible to make up one's own illustrations, or construct one's own sentences to suit a particular child using the construction rules given in the manual.

In conclusion

The encouragement of language development has many facets: creating situations (as in a nursery) where language use is demanded or made possible, where natural language models are continuously available; providing opportunities as in visits or limited excursions where the environment's novelty or ambiguity prompts the child to comment or question. But added on to all these, for the mentally handicapped or language retarded child, is the need for some well-structured and *focused* language teaching. Any successful remediation is likely to arise out of the interaction of these (and other) factors.

The Evolution of a Portage-based Core Curriculum

Jan Asplett, Moya Evans, Gillian Haslegrave, Sue Lamport, Pauline Preston, Liz Rook and Meriel Wilkins

The authors are members of staff at The Willows Special Nursery, Portsmouth, Hampshire.

The Willows Nursery is a recognized special school in Portsmouth. It has been open for nearly ten years and was purpose-built to cater for pre-school children. We have been involved with the project for some four years now, although our interest has been in the use of it as a means of structured teaching in the nursery. We hope that this paper will give readers the flavour of the considerations and constraints in using the Portage teaching technology within a school setting.

A number of problems have stopped us from involving parents in the way in which they would normally participate in a Portage project, not least of which are the problems of transport to the outlying areas from which children are drawn. However, our involvement with Portage has led us to consider very carefully the curriculum we offer our children and to use the Portage checklist to work out a curriculum consisting of clear steps which we would like our children to follow. This means we are in a position to inform parents fully of where their child is starting and what we wish him or her to achieve.

Arrangements in the nursery

Currently we have 35 children on roll, 25 of whom attend at any one time. About one third of all the children attend for a full week, while for the remainder arrangements are kept flexible. Children are brought to us by bus in the morning and returned in the evening and volunteer drivers help us transport children who either arrive or leave at lunch time.

These children are referred by educational psychologists and tend to show a wide variety of needs; a large number of them need help with language.

The nursery is divided into three main areas. One is known as the 'wet' room and lives up to its name. Here messy, creative activities are carried out. In another part of the building, there is a large play area which can be halved by the use of a heavy screen; with the screen in use one half is almost fully carpeted, lending itself to quiet activity, while the other contains a large climbing frame catering for more mobile and energetic activities. Our staff consists of three teachers and three nursery nurses, who work in pairs. There is also a head teacher. We are assisted by a speech therapist who comes in for five out of our ten sessions – it is hoped that in the future this provision will be increased. We are fortunate in being adjacent to a school clinic where we have ready access to the clinic's provisions such as a physiotherapist, health visitor representative and the Schools' Psychological Service.

Development of the Portage-based curriculum

Initially Portage was used by one teacher and one nursery nurse, working with a group of less able children who attend part time. The advantages of the scheme in teaching new skills became more and more apparent; however, this group was becoming separate from the rest of the school and was beginning to lose out on interactions with the other children.

In the autumn of 1981 it seemed that children with more severe learning problems were being referred to us and it was decided to move from group teaching to an open-plan, team-teaching arrangement using Portage-type teaching programmes as a basis for our curriculum.

At the start of 1982 two teachers planned full Portage programmes, consisting of three tasks using activity charts carried out with the help of the nursery nurses. The other teachers monitored and taught skills to the remaining more able children and planned a series of precise objectives and teaching methods based on the cognitive items from the Portage checklist. Broadly speaking, the cognitive checklist was broken down under the main headings of Matching and Sorting, Colour, Spatial, Number, Shape, Concepts, Memory plus graded puzzles recorded on a separate chart. All work on this curriculum scheme was monitored fortnightly by a staff meeting at which an educational psychologist attended.

Activity charts are filed weekly in individual folders and information summarized on a termly sheet for quicker reference. Full Portage checklists were completed and sent on to the child's next school. For the more able children only, cognitive and fine motor aspects of the checklists were forwarded to their next school. Our experience shows that many tasks needed to be broken down into small steps and as staff members found that this needed to be done, the steps they decided upon were filed in a task analysis book so that other staff working on the same objective could benefit from their experience.

This method of organizing continued for two terms only – we realized that a divide was emerging between those receiving this help and some of the more able children. At this point we began a second revision of the Portage checklist in order to provide a structured curriculum that would encompass both these groups. This also enabled us to produce our own assessment pack, that would be completed by educational psychologists before children were sent to us, that served as a guide as to the suitability of the child and at what point he or she should begin in the curriculum.

In the autumn of 1982, with 39 children attending, each teacher had a mixed activity group and a nursery teacher supported all activities. Now every child had three curriculum schemes to follow, which were cognitive, fine motor skills and language. The less able child worked towards the acquisition of skills, while the more able were taught to generalize the skills they often already had, through the use of a wide variety of equipment. Although we were team-teaching to agreed objectives, staff decided upon their own methods. However, by Easter, 1983, there was recognition of the need to standardize teaching methods as a result of group discussions which revealed inconsistencies between the approach of different teachers. Thus, fine motor tasks were the first to be reviewed, additional task analyses were written and a manual was collated for general use in 'table-top' teaching, working with a child on the agreed objectives. Individual fine motor activity charts now gave way to descriptions of activities to be carried out in groups: cognitive charts were still used on an individual basis while task analyses were reviewed and a similar file produced.

Changes in the organization of teaching

The discussion previously mentioned led to a definition being made between teaching children individually in a group setting and teaching them in a group. It was agreed that group teaching would particularly benefit those children due to transfer to school in the near future and those who were intellectually more able. Ultimately the decision was to have a core of group teaching from which children would be withdrawn for individual support using activity charts if they were found to be having difficulties. A number of possible activities for group teaching were discussed, including specific games and some more general activities.

At the start of the autumn term, 1983, we organized class teaching in three separate groups, each in the care of one teacher and one nursery nurse. At any one time we would be responsible for eight or nine children of varying ability within the range catered for by the school. This reorganization was intended to enable the teachers to implement group teaching; consequently equipment was distributed on as equal a basis as possible within the nursery. Groups now rotate within the three working areas to provide all the experience necessary. The teaching of children individually while in a group setting for fine motor skills and use of puzzles and the recording in these areas of progress proceeds as before.

The teaching of particular cognitive skills in groups by small individual steps presented some difficulties and has resulted in various skills being brought together to form a more general developmental progression of learning activities in particular areas. Quite often we have found it important to form sub-groups of pupils at a similar level. The recording of children's progress in this area varies from group to group and it is clear that some standardization will be necessary.

Derbyshire Language Scheme as part of the school curriculum

The Derbyshire Language Scheme was established in the nursery before Portage was introduced. Whilst Portage was being adapted to our needs we looked at the possibility of the Derbyshire scheme being used alongside. Both have a structured approach with identifiable objectives which are aimed to be achieved within a short period. The Derbyshire has small structured steps and when bridging from one level to the next, activities need to be broken down in a systematic way, similar to the process of task analysis.

Prior to the introduction of Portage, approximately 75 per cent of the children were taught twice weekly in groups working at specific levels. However, the varying times of attendance for both the children and the speech therapist led to some 25 per cent being seen individually by the speech therapist on a weekly basis and then being discussed with the teacher.

With the introduction of the Portage curriculum we increased the number of children on individual programmes to approximately 75 per cent and the remainder was taught in groups – this resulted in the majority of children receiving specific language teaching daily from the nursery staff as well as their other Portage activities. The individual programme was monitored by the speech therapist who had weekly contact with each child and discussed their programme with their teachers.

Each term the population of the nursery changes and it is often necessary to alter the balance of group and individual teaching. As with Portage it is important to be flexible in the approach to the teaching organization. For example, this term with the introduction of class groups we find it possible to organize groups within each class and fewer individual programmes are required.

For recording both group and individual Derbyshire activities, we are using an adaptation of the Portage activity chart (see Figures 1 and 2). Our experience suggests that the similar approaches of both the Derbyshire scheme and the Portage teaching technique link very successfully.

Conclusions

As you will see from what has been written, the school has gained through a number of changes in curriculum, teaching method and overall organization in response to the needs of its pupils. In many ways it is impossible to be sure of reaching a perfect solution to the problems of our children. Nevertheless some general indicators do emerge. The use of Portage in setting and breaking down goals into small steps has proved a useful foundation for our structured curriculum. Now that a clear direction to the work being done has been established, it is obviously crucially important to obtain as effective an organization as possible to ensure efficient teaching and to maximize impact on the children in our care.

Figure 1: Adaptation of Portage activity chart (Derbyshire Language Scheme): group work

WILLOWS NURSERY **DERBYSHIRE LANGUAGE SCHEME** **GROUP WORK**

WEEK BEGINNING 19 March 1984 TEACHER E.R.

GROUP A LEVEL 2 WORD COMPREHENSION

STRUCTURE BEING TAUGHT
transfer of object to person

MATERIALS 2 toys: doll and monkey.
3 movable toys: car, boat, train.

DLS No. A2 : 5

METHOD
Ask the child to push the *boat* to *dolly*.
Repeat with two other combinations of toys in each session.

NAME	RESULTS	SESSION 1	RESULTS	SESSION 2
Chris	✓	car → monkey	(✓)	train → dolly
	(✓)	boat → dolly	✓	car → monkey
	✓	car → dolly	✓	boat → dolly
Jim	✓	boat → dolly	✓	boat → dolly
	✓	train → dolly	✓	boat → monkey
	✓	boat → dolly	✓	car → monkey
Mike	✓	car → dolly	✓	train → dolly
	✓	boat → dolly	✓	car → monkey
	(✓)	train → monkey	✓	car → dolly

Record: ✓ Success (✓) Success with extra help ✗ Incorrect response

Figure 2: Adaptation of Portage activity chart (Derbyshire Language Scheme): individual work

WILLOWS NURSERY DERBYSHIRE LANGUAGE SCHEME INDIVIDUAL WORK

CHILD'S NAME: John *WEEK BEGINNING:* 19/3/84

DLS NO: A3 : 8

STRUCTURE BEING TAUGHT: Action on an object

COMPREHENSION/EXPRESSION

MATERIALS: Doll/teddy
toothbrush, hairbrush, flannel, shampoo

METHOD:
Comprehension: Ask child to 'wash dolly's hands' etc.
Expression: Ask child to describe adult actions with above items.

	COMPREHENSION	EXPRESSION
MONDAY	brush teddy's hair wash dolly's feet wash teddy's hands	brush hair dolly hair brush dolly hair (imitation) wash teddy – hair
TUESDAY	brush dolly's teeth wash teddy's tummy wash dolly's hands	dolly teeth – brush wash teddy face
WEDNESDAY	wash teddy's hair brush dolly's teeth brush teddy's hair	wash hair – teddy wash teddy hair brush hair
THURSDAY		
FRIDAY		

South Wales Early Language Research Project: the development of a practicable, assessment-linked language training curriculum for use with the handicapped child.*

Clare Jones, John Clements, Christina Evans, Kate Osborne and Graham Upton

The authors include practising clinical psychologists, a research assistant in psychology, and lecturers in psychology and education.

For any child, the development of an effective language is perhaps the most important and most difficult learning objective. Language is crucial to communication and the development of advanced thinking processes. It is used to guide the person's own behaviour, and to affect the behaviour of others. Research suggesting 'critical periods' for language development (Lennenberg, 1967) urges provision of adequate stimulation at the right time.

The model we adopted was similar to that of the Portage system devised for working with pre-school handicapped children and their families (Shearer and Shearer, 1972). This involves skill targets being set for each child, on which the parents work daily for short periods in between the weekly visits of the 'home adviser'. It incorporates modelling and feedback procedures. The curriculum is derived from detailed developmental checklists, each item having an

---

* Reprinted here with kind permission of the authors and of the editor of *Mental Handicap*, **11**, 1, 30–32, 1983.

associated card giving ideas on how to teach the particular skill. Pilot work with the system in the UK (Revill and Blunden, 1979; Clements *et al.*, 1980) suggested that the system was practicable, very popular with parents, and accelerated the child's rate of development.

Basic issues

A growing mass of literature looks at 'normal' language development, assesses training methods and philosophies, and identifies key areas of development. Although many grey areas of knowledge remain (Bell, 1979), there is a thread of agreement on basic issues which can now be picked out from the current literature, namely:

1. Language training must take into account developmental norms, not only in the sphere of language but also in the fields of cognitive and motor development (Stevens, 1981).
2. There is a need to develop language teaching from the rather simplistic, vocabulary enrichment approach to include the development of syntax – the rules of language (Bell, 1979). Linked in with this is the essential premise that the meaning must be taught with the word to enable the thought!
3. Assessments of the 'standardized test score', 'fixed-item' kind are not appropriate for the development of language remediation programmes. Assessment and remediation programmes must be developed and evaluated in parallel.
4. For the handicapped child, structured language teaching is the method of choice (Fenn, 1976).

Development of the Early Language Profile (ELP)

In a search of the published literature for a practicable assessment-linked language training programme, suitable for use by parents or teachers of the mentally handicapped child, the programmes offered present difficulties and deficits. Many of the assessments lack flexibility and do not allow the unique pattern of the individual child to show through prior to planning training. Often, inadequate attention is paid to the comprehension of language and pre-language skills. Syntax and semantics are inadequately covered. Some detailed assessments have been described as 'presenting formidable problems' (Bell, 1979), even to trained teachers of the severely handicapped, and tend to be complex and unwieldy.

It is these deficiencies and gaps which inspired the three-year Early Language Research Project in South Wales. The specific aims were:

> to develop a comprehensive language assessment to act as a curriculum guide for the teaching programme – the Early Language Profile (ELP);
>
> to develop a range of teaching strategies to enhance progress through the curriculum;
>
> to examine the individual progress of each child for information about the rate and order of acquisition of skills;
>
> to implement and evaluate a home-based training programme by examining: (i) language development progress between groups; (ii) progress within an experimental group.

The first stage of the research was the development of the Early Language Profile (ELP), which was subsequently piloted at a school for severely mentally handicapped children before the experimental phase began.

Teaching strategies used

Training procedures were based on the underlying premise that language is acquired because a child is born with systems that predispose him to speak, and because his environment encourages him to do so. The training content and methods were considered carefully before being put into practice with the experimental groups. Reynell (1973) pointed out the danger of improving language skills without improving the language process as such. In consequence, the programme incorporated representational play and use of symbols as well as aspects of motor development, and the training cards were designed with a constant nod towards the work of Piaget!

It is the degree of handicap, the slowness of learning, which must determine the teaching method used. For the severely handicapped or developmentally very young child spontaneous play and trial and error learning with modelling is not sufficient to train new skills or processes. For these children, operant training procedures are essential; but just as essential is the necessity to broaden the content of what is taught, and to build in the process of generalization through spontaneous imitation, parallel conversation, and play-related language.

As a result of this, for each item on the ELP a set of ideas for training was developed with appropriate training aids.

It was felt that a truer assessment of the child's capabilities could be obtained in the natural environment, so training was provided through a home visiting service. This method also increased the involvement of the parents in the children's daily training programmes.

Evaluation of the scheme

The experimental phase consisted of assessment over approximately 18 months in Gwent using the ELP in conjunction with a regular home training service based on the Portage model. In order to validate the work over as wide a range of ability levels as possible, two experimental groups were used. One was a pre-school group comprising six children, three boys and three girls. Their ages ranged from two months to 25 months at the start of intervention. Their developmental quotients on the Ruth Griffiths Developmental Scales ranged from 40 to 107, and their mental ages from 2.8 months to 12 months. Four children had Down's Syndrome, one was cerebral palsied, and the other was said to have 'general developmental delay'. The other experimental group included nine school-age children, five of whom had Down's Syndrome and four of whom had been diagnosed as having 'general developmental delay'. Their ages at the start of the scheme ranged from five years two months to nine years eight months. Their intelligence quotients ranged from 'less than 30' up to 61. All the children were at least at the one-word vocabulary stage. These groups were compared with other groups drawn from neighbouring geographical areas, who did not receive the same home visiting service.

The evaluation was based on within-group comparisons using the ELP itself (for example, see Tables 1 and 2), a parental interview, and between-group comparisons on standarized test scores. The statistical analysis used enabled us to investigate pre-intervention, post-intervention and change scores, allowing for the effects of age and intelligence.

The comparison of standardized test scores confirms language improvement for the children in both experimental groups.

Table 1: Summary of ELP assessments for school-age experimental group

	Non verbal	Response to sounds	Simple commands	Vocabulary	More complex syntax	Motor movements	Speech sounds	Babbling	Vocabulary	Single words	Two words	Three words	More complex syntax
Child 15	√	√	√	√+	√+	√	√	√	√+	√	+	+	+
Child 14	√	√	√	√+	√+	√	√	√	√+	√	√+	√+	√+
Child 13	√	√	√	√+	√+	√	√	√	√+	√	√+	√+	√+
Child 12	√	√	√	√+	√+	√	√	√	√+	√	√+	√+	+
Child 11	√	√	√	√+	√+	√	√	√	√+	√	√+	√+	√+
Child 10	√	√	√	√+	√+	√	√	√	√+	√	√	√+	√+
Child 9	√	√	√	√+	√+	√	√	√	√+	√	√	+	√+
Child 8	√	√	√	√+	√+	√	√	√	√+	√	+	+	+
Child 7	√	√	√	√+	√+	√	√	√	√+	√	√+	√+	√+

Key
√ items recorded at initial assessment
√+ items recorded during intervention
\+ items recorded at the end of intervention

However, it does not confirm that their progress was any greater than that made by comparable groups of children who did not receive similar training. Possible reasons for this are discussed in the full report of the research (Clements *et al.*, 1980). The most likely explanation is that the assessment items were not sensitive enough to register the differential changes. Details of all the analyses and results are published in full in the research report.

Table 2: Summary of ELP assessments for pre-school experimental group

	Non verbal	Language comprehension				Language production							
		Response to sounds	Simple commands	Vocabulary	More complex syntax	Motor movements	Speech sounds	Babbling	Vocabulary	Single words	Two words	Three words	More complex syntax
Child 6	√+	√	√+	√+		√+	√+	√+	+	+			
Child 5	√+	√	√+	√+		√+	√+	√+					
Child 4	√+	√	√+	√+		√+	√+	√+	√				
Child 3	√+	√	√+	√+		√	√	√	+	+			
Child 2	√+	√	√+	√+		√+	√+	√+	√+	+	+		
Child 1	√+	√+	+	+		√+	√+	+	+				

Key
√ items recorded at initial assessment
√+ items recorded during intervention
\+ items recorded at the end of intervention

The interviews with parents reflected much enthusiasm for the language training offered. Many parents commented that the scheme helped pinpoint the deficits in their child's language and they appreciated having specific, recordable training ideas, couched in familiar everyday terms, on a regular basis. They also welcomed the advice on choice of toys and games for use in the stimulation of various stages of language. At the same time the home advisers who piloted the scheme found it extremely useful to have a structured and comprehensive assessment (the ELP) from which to work, with concurrent guides to training at each step. The study was unusual in the breadth of its approach to language development, and the extended period of time over which it was evaluated. In this kind of applied research, however, there are many methodological problems so that the results are not as clear-cut as findings obtained in controlled laboratory situations. Nevertheless, it was the specific intention of the researchers, who work in the clinical psychology and educational fields, to keep within a framework that would be relevant to staff engaged in practical service provisions.

The percentage of tasks that were subsequently recorded as successfully achieved reflects the value and merit of the training guides that were evolved during the study.

To conclude

The research succeeded in producing a comprehensive language assessment profile (the ELP) and a well-tried set of training cards, utilizing the expertise of five professionals experienced in work with language delayed mentally handicapped children.

The full report of the research is available from Clare Jones, Principal Psychologist, at St. Cadoc's Hospital, Caerleon, Gwent, price £2.00 at the time of printing. Cheques payable to Gwent Health Authority.

The *Early Language Profile and Training Kit* are available from Drake Educational Associates.

Portage Initiatives

Electrifying Portage

Dr Charles Palmer and Dr Steve Huggett

Charles Palmer works with the Coventry School Psychological Service, and Steve Huggett with the Hampshire School Psychological Service.

'Thinking means connecting things and stops if they cannot be connected.'

G.K. Chesterton.

If a historian in the future was looking back over Special Education in the Seventies and Eighties, we suspect that there would be two major trends which would figure predominantly: the growth in the application of the Portage teaching technology and the rapid increase in the use of microcomputers in special schools. It is therefore perhaps inevitable that these two major developments would meet. We do not know if this project is the first marriage between microcomputers and Portage, but we are clear that it will not be the last.

Although the work we are describing does not directly involve parents, it does have implications for their part in Portage. If a partnership with parents means anything, it rests on both partners having access to the same information: microcomputers should make life easier.

Microcomputers in Special Education

The growth in the use of microcomputers in school in Britain over the last two years or so has been phenomenal. For example, in Hampshire in 1980 there were approximately 120 microcomputers in operation in schools, whereas by the middle of 1984 there was somewhere in excess of 2,000. There has also been particular interest in this new teaching aid in schools for children with special needs. Mr. Kenneth Baker, at the time of writing Minister for Information Technology, recently announced a £2.5 million microelectronics budget for special schools and there are indications that the lion's share of this allocation will be with schools that were formerly categorized as ESN(M) (*Times Educational Supplement*, 9 September 1983).

However, the current application of microcomputers in special education has been characterized by children themselves interfacing with computers. Thus, the microcomputer has been used very directly to teach children skills which have previously required a great deal of direct teaching time. On the other hand, we know of very little work in which microcomputers are being used to help *teachers* in the day-to-day requirements of record keeping and curriculum development. We find this surprising because in the special schools in which we work there seems to be a very real need for this function and this was especially pronounced in the special nursery in which this project was set. It is worth stressing therefore that the problems that the current project sought to tackle were present before the microcomputer arrived. We feel that this is a point worth stressing as it is very easy for microcomputers to be seen by staff as a solution in search of a problem. If the latter situation applies then the use of the microcomputer and the work of the teacher carry on in parallel without one influencing the other. The connection between the two becomes tenuous and unhelpful and we were interested to see that this problem does not only apply to education.

Therefore, we feel it is important to outline the context in which the computer in this project was applied as, in more senses than one, the needs of the school came first. We will outline the curriculum development which has been going on in the nursery school for the past two years (for more details see Brosnan and Huggett, 1984 and Asplett *et al.* in this volume) before we detail how the microcomputer helped this process.

Curriculum at The Willows nursery school

The Willows nursery school in Portsmouth caters for the needs of something like 30 to 40 3–5-year-old children who have various special needs. At any one time there are approximately 25 children in the nursery which is staffed by the head teacher, three teachers, three nursery nurses and a half-time speech therapist. There is also frequent and regular input from the School Psychological Service, whose offices are next door to the nursery.

The Willows opened in 1973 and at the outset the head teacher was faced with meeting the needs of three broad groups of children: firstly, children with marked language delay, secondly, children with behavioural problems and thirdly, a few children who were severely handicapped. At the outset, the staff realized it was essential to chart the progress of the children at the nursery as, with such diverse needs, it was possible for some children to 'slip through the net' if their progress was not monitored closely. Thus, children had an initial assessment on arrival at The Willows and there were regular staff meetings to monitor their progress. By 1979, following several staff and organizational changes, it had become increasingly difficult to integrate the less able children into the mainstream of teaching being carried out at the nursery. Therefore individual Portage programmes were applied to meet the needs of these children with more severe learning difficulties. By the autumn of 1981 there had been a change in the intake of The Willows such that there was an increasing number of severely handicapped children. Furthermore, there had been staff changes which had resulted in a new teacher's being appointed and a new speech therapist working at The Willows. The second author also joined at this time as a psychologist for the nursery. These changes necessitated a major rethink of the curriculum and it was decided to use the *Portage Guide to Early Education* as a starting point for development of the *whole curriculum* instead of just using it for work with a few individual children. Thus in January 1982 an inservice training day was organized to initiate the use of the Portage teaching technology for all children at the nursery.

The organization of the Portage curriculum at The Willows.

All children at The Willows have individual programmes which are monitored either by using activity charts or more general records indicating progress along objectives derived from the *Portage Guide to Early Education*. Each child is designated three targets for the week, one item from the cognitive section of the checklist, one dealing with fine motor skills and one language objective. Work was generally done on an individual basis but there was concern that this was a very time-consuming way of teaching. A time sampling exercise was carried out at The Willows which indicated that on average children received something like 10–12 minutes' individual teaching per day and that even this seemingly modest commitment left very little time for group activity.

Curriculum items were sequenced on two levels. On the first level items from the Portage checklists were ordered so that earlier skills prepare children for the teaching of later skills. Although the staff derived these sequences independently they are essentially similar to those carried out by Jill Gardener in Walsall (See Gardener 1980).

However, the gaps between items in the first level sequences are often very large and this has necessitated a task analysis being performed on individual items to break them down into more negotiable steps. Thus a large number of checklist items have been task analysed, each step given a notation and the sequence filed away for future reference. These task analyses are subject to constant revision in the light of teaching experience.

It is important to note at this point that language teaching in The Willows derives from the Derbyshire Language Scheme and on the whole does not use the language section of the Portage checklist. However, the Derbyshire scheme dovetails very well with the Portage system as it is also a very structured sequential system. These features have enabled the same management procedures to be applied to language work as for the Portage activity, even though they derive from different sources.

The sequence of Portage teaching

On entry to The Willows, each child is screened in key Portage areas selected from Portage checklists. This enables teaching to take place more quickly than the lengthy baselining procedure would allow. It was interesting to note that increasingly this initial screening is being done before the children arrive at The Willows as the local educational psychologists are now using a derivation of the screening procedure that was being used in The Willows.

Following this initial screening, children are set short-term targets on a weekly basis which relate to long-term targets which are set on a termly basis. Progress is reviewed at fortnightly meetings, chaired by the educational psychologist with the head teacher, the teachers, nursery nurses and the speech therapist. These meetings have a dual function in that they not only monitor individual progress but also serve as a venue for decisions to be made about curriculum development within the nursery. Thus, for example, curriculum discussion concerning particular task analyses or teaching methods may be instigated by discussion of the problems of a particular child.

The final feature of the monitoring system involves an end of term review of all the skills attained by each child so that this can be used to plan future teaching targets and also to evaluate the performance of the curriculum for the term.

Objectives-based curricula are time-consuming for teachers

This fine-grained monitoring of children's progress through objectives demands a great deal of time from teaching staff.

This work is very demanding both in terms of monitoring individual children and also the consequent curriculum development that this implies. With respect to individual children, activity charts have to be written and the child's progress monitored on a weekly and termly basis. This throws up considerable amounts of information which have a direct bearing on the curriculum. Task analyses are revised in the light of experience and the efficacy of teaching methods reviewed. Thus the problem for the staff at The Willows was not only to gather information but also to relate this information in a number of different ways so that teaching could be informed by experience. This necessarily involved large amounts of paper being collated and information derived so that it could be put to use. Essentially what was needed was a system whereby information gathered in one context was automatically related to others. Enter the micro chip.

Using a microcomputer at The Willows

Our aim then, was to investigate the possible role of a microcomputer in the twin processes of curriculum development and record keeping.

The project ran to a tight time scale, and lasted only ten months from start to finish.

October 1982	:	Initial development work and discussion with The Willows staff.
November 1982	:	Research proposal sent to Tandy UK. Tandy agree to provide hardware.
December 1982	:	Computer arrives, familiarization with operating systems.
January – February 1983	:	Software written.
March – May 1983	:	Computer used in school.
June – July 1983	:	Evaluation data collected.

The early development work and discussion with The Willows staff was crucial to the success of the project. We aimed *not* to provide the staff with our idea of what was the best record keeping system, but to use the computer to mimic the procedures which were already in use in the school. Not only is this approach common sense in that the school's experience of keeping records is built in, but has the advantage that the teachers are aware in a broad sense of what the machine will do.

The way in which a complex curriculum such as the Willows' operates is an area which receives little attention. While there is much talk of developing new curricula and teaching methods, much less is heard about how they should be implemented. We have introduced the term 'curriculum management' to refer to those processes concerned with the operation of a curriculum, and discuss the area in more detail elsewhere (Palmer and Huggett, 1984). Clearly, we could not develop a computer programme until a clear picture of the the Willows' curriculum management procedures was available.

The only area which was not included in the present project was the initial assessment. It would not have been appropriate, given the limited time scale.

Briefly, then, we knew that the programme would be required to:

1) Keep details of curriculum items and task analyses of items.
2) Keep records for each child of:
   a) items already achieved,
   b) items set as long-term targets,
   c) items set as short-term targets.
3) Allow teachers to record the results of teaching, present short-term targets, and set new targets for the future.
4) Produce activity charts for present short-term targets.
5) To provide summary information on the performance of both individual children and the curriculum as a whole.

Technical details

Tandy provided the following hardware on loan:

TRS-80 III microcomputer with twin SSDD disk drives
DWP-410 Daisywheel printer.

For those interested, the Model III has since been replaced by the more powerful Model IV.

Two kinds of information were stored on disk. First, details of the curriculum, and second, details of each child's attainments and future targets. Information of both kinds was structured as records within a file. Within a curriculum file, each record held details of one particular item from the Portage checklist. Further files held details of task analyses that had been prepared for particular items. Similarly, within child files, each record contained details of one particular Portage item, and included such details as date started and finished, teaching method used, whether the task analysis was used or not, and so on.

Further, a single letter attached to each record denoted the status of that record, as follows:

T : Long-term target
S : Short-term target
A : Attained this term
R : Attained last term
P : Attained more than a term ago
B : Abandoned this term
C : Abandoned last term or earlier.

The programme automatically updated the item status as was appropriate. For example, as the teacher recorded the results of teaching current short-term target items, status was changed from 'S' to 'A' if the item was attained, to 'B' if it was abandoned, or left as 'S' if more teaching was needed.

This system ensured that the programme never lost track of items in a particular child's file. For example, let us imagine that a teacher records for young Johnny 'Motor 82' as a termly target item. When she comes to set short-term targets for Johnny, she will always be reminded that 'Motor 82' is there for consideration. When she chooses, its status is changed from 'T' to 'S' and again, when she records the results of teaching to other objectives she will be prompted for the results of teaching 'Motor 82' until she records that the item is attained or abandoned. Further details are available in Palmer (1984).

Software development

This was carried out by the first author, a task which he would not have undertaken had he recognized the complexity and difficulty at the start! Many long hours were spent staring at a television screen in the middle of the night. These comments are made not to engender sympathy, but to warn those interested in starting similar projects. Had this programme been developed commercially its cost would have been roughly three times the cost of the hardware.

The moral of the story is that when putting together a proposal for this kind of work, the major item is not hardware, but software. It is unfortunately much easier to obtain resources for hardware than for software, and yet the latter is crucial. Computer programmes do not write themselves (yet!)

Implementation

During early discussion with staff at The Willows, Meriel Wilkins, deputy head, volunteered to use the system with the ten children for whom she was responsible. Moya Evans, teacher, also agreed to become involved on the curriculum side.

The early stage of implementation required a great deal of information to be typed into the computer. The authors would like to thank Meriel and Moya for the long hours put in to get the system 'off the ground'.

The introduction of the use of the system was staged over five weeks, and proceeded via a set of clearly defined objectives. Early objectives were as follows:

> to record previous records and long term targets for two children
>
> to record details of ten Portage items and associated task analyses.

The system gradually become operational as each objective was achieved, and attainment of the final objective implied that

1) ten children had previous records, long and short-term targets recorded for them
2) teaching results were recorded for all ten children
3) thirty curriculum items and task analyses had been recorded.

The short-term nature of the project meant that the curriculum information that was stored was necessarily limited. Had the project continued, this could have been built up gradually.

System Functions

When the computer is switched on, the system asks for the date, and then displays one or two 'menus' of available functions. Details are as follows.

INDIVIDUAL FUNCTIONS

(1) Initial assessment. This involves recording what the child can already do. Included here, as well as the Portage items the child can accomplish on entry, is general information about the child, his or her date of birth, and frequency of attendance.

(2) Setting teaching targets for the term. The school where development took place found it difficult to work from the Portage checklist as a whole, and decided to categorize items they were likely to want to teach into eleven curriculum areas (e.g., writing, concepts, memory, eye/hand co-ordination, manipulation). The computer asks the teacher to set termly targets for a child in each curriculum area. For each area, the teacher is presented with what the child has achieved some time ago, what he or she achieved last term, and any targets not achieved last term. The teacher uses this information to set new targets. She may well decide not to set any targets for a child in a particular area of course. After each area has been considered, the computer presents a summary of all the termly targets which have been set. The teacher has the option of making further changes.

(3) Setting short-term targets. Short-term targets are the items which a child is being taught or will be taught, over a two-week period. Again, the process is done for each curriculum area in turn. Each time, the teacher is presented with what the child has already achieved this term, what termly target items have not yet been taught, and any short-term target items which have not been finished (from the previous short-term target). Again, once the process has been completed for each curriculum area, the teacher is presented with a summary statement of all the short-term targets which she has set. The option of making further changes is then available.

This process is not as long-winded as it sounds; most short-term targets only contain about three items.

(4) Recording teaching results. In this part of the programme, once the teacher has typed in the child's name, the computer displays each short-term target item in turn. The computer offers the teacher a choice of three possible outcomes. First, the child has successfully completed the item; second, the child is still working on the item; and third, the item has been abandoned as being too hard for the child.

The computer then asks for information appropriate to the outcome. For example, if the child is still working on the item, the computer tells the teacher when the child started work on the item, and asks the teacher if she wants to change the teaching method. It also offers the teacher the chance of adding information to the notes concerning the child's performance on the item. Other teaching outcomes result in the computer going through different procedures.

Further individual functions deal with output of information from the system.

(5) Looking at termly targets. A list is provided as a printout.

(6) Looking at short-term targets. Current short-term targets are displayed.

(7) Looking at what the child has done this term. This provides a list of achievements, short-term targets and long-term targets. This function may well prove to be of particular interest to parents.

(8) End of term summary. The computer provides a printout giving details of all the items achieved during the term.

SCHOOL-WIDE FUNCTIONS

(1) Record teaching methods and materials for a particular item. This information would be printed out on an activity chart for a particular child doing this item.

(2) Recording or changing a task analysis. Once the set of steps is recorded, it may be added to either in the middle or at the end. This information might also appear on an activity chart, where the teacher was teaching a particular step.

(3) Recording a sequence of items in a particular curriculum area. Each item has a curriculum area number within the data base. Once these are allocated (and this has not yet been done) the computer will be able to output items in a curriculum area in the appropriate teaching order.

(4) Looking at a task analysis. The teachers required two formats for task analyses. These have been provided. In each, however, the steps appear sequentially.

(5) Looking at the details. Teachers may look up the teaching methods and materials appropriate to teaching a particular item.

(6) End of term summary. Here the computer adds up the teaching episodes of each item across all children and provides summary information. The information concerns teaching methods used, and average number of half-day sessions taken to teach the item. The information content of this part of the programme was carefully worked out with the educational psychologist. It was hoped to avoid presenting information which could not be acted upon if necessary.

Evaluation

Two questions were posed. First, did the machine do what we hoped it would? Second, was this set of functions useful to the school?

With respect to the first question, the set of objectives governing the introduction of the system to the school has already been referred to. Early items in the sequence involved building up the information base required, while later targets referred to the increasing number of children for whom both long and short-term targets were being set and teaching results recorded, on a regular basis. The gradual development of the system's use was thus continuously monitored. Furthermore, part of the system required users to record what they had been doing with the system (unfortunately attracting some unprintable comments!) and whether any problems had arisen. This, taken alongside regular, weekly contact between users and developer, ensured that any bugs in the system or awkward operating procedures could be corrected as quickly as possible.

The second question was approached directly, by asking all school staff for comments. The broad picture emerging looked like this.

Deficits:
1) Requires a great deal of work in the early stages.
2) Requires some time to learn how to use.
3) Creates some worries over the general problem of the confidentiality of computer records.

Assets:
1) Printed output extremely useful (e.g., task analyses, activity charts).
2) Acted as a spur to curriculum development within the school.
3) Benefits beginning to be felt only towards the end of the project.

The general feeling was that the system had a great deal of potential, and that a much longer period was required for full evaluation so that the early work required in establishing the information base could be offset against later gains in efficiency. Fuller details can be found in Palmer (1984).

Conclusions

The development of curricula designed to meet special educational needs has resulted in a rapid expansion of the 'clerical' side of teaching. Precise records must be kept, and detailed curricula must be reviewed and updated. We have termed the general area 'curriculum management' (see Palmer and Huggett, 1984, for more details).

This project was aimed at testing the feasibility of using a microcomputer to relieve teachers of some of the clerical burden associated with managing the curriculum. We strongly believe that the project was successful to the extent that it provides enough optimism to support more extensive work in the area. Indeed, the first author has such a project under way at a nursery for children with special needs in Coventry.

The area will no doubt develop rapidly, but we would like to offer some comments on the experience we have already gained.

First, we believe that it is crucial that software is individually tailored to the curriculum management procedures used by the particular school. Schools, as well as children, have individual needs. On the other hand, there are bound to be a core of common procedures, and types of information to be stored, between schools. The extent of this core will only become apparent from further experience. Again, the arrival of a microcomputer, and the resultant necessity for a school to specify exactly what it does do in the area of curriculum management, would seem to act as a spur to people getting together and examining whether current practices can be improved.

Second, the hardware needed to support this kind of project is beyond what is currently available in schools. The amount of data which has to be stored necessitates the use of multiple disk drives, and a high-quality printer is also required. Expert advice is needed to decide precisely what kind of hardware is needed, but our experience suggests that total cost is likely to be in the two or three thousand pounds bracket, at 1983 prices.

We have already mentioned the importance of provision for the development of the software. It is important to add here that access to the expertise should be maintained for some time after the system has come into operation.

Most applications of Portage are of course home-based rather than school-based, and a system such as this is not going to be economically justifiable to services given their present limited size. Moreover, the needs of a home teaching service are very different from the needs of a school, and concern for curriculum management procedures are certainly less central. We feel that the system is best applied to school settings, and the curriculum is of course not limited to the Portage materials. The system would be applicable to any special needs curriculum that is specified in terms of precise objectives.

Finally, in accordance with the book's theme, some thoughts about parents. In what is essentially an attempt to aid the way a school handles information about learning, parents should be enabled to see benefits. Directly, the system should provide excellent access for parents to see what their children are working on and progress that has been made. They should also be aware of benefits indirectly, via a hopefully improved service offered to them and their children.

Using Portage with the Severely Mentally and Visually Handicapped

Pamela Courtney

Pamela Courtney teaches at the Ellen Terry and Brooklands School.

The Ellen Terry and Brooklands School* caters for severely mentally handicapped, blind and partially sighted children. There are nine classes with an age range of two to nineteen-year-olds.

As far back as 1957 it was felt that most of our present training methods for the mentally handicapped child needed re-thinking as they sometimes fostered the kind of behaviours they were trying over-zealously to correct. This thinking led to a three-year study which demonstrated that, when placed in a stimulating, protective and emotionally warm environment, severely mentally handicapped children react in much the same way as young, normal children. Their development proceeds through the same sequences, though at a much slower pace, and it was also evident that a greater development of verbal ability and social behaviour occurred when the children were cared for in *small family groups*. A film entitled '*Mentally Handicapped Children Growing-up*' was made about this work and it spurred demand for new approaches to handicapped children. The Warnock Report is the latest in a long line of policy documents working out the implications of the work done by Dr. J. Tizard with the Brooklands Experimental Unit (Tizard, 1961). Therefore, our aim, over the years, has been to provide the best methods possible to help our children. As can be seen from the following our methods are continually being reviewed and revised and are clearly influenced by Portage.

---

* Later re-named the Brooklands School for Visually Handicapped Children with Severe Learning Difficulties.

How we were introduced to Portage and our revisions

We were introduced to Portage by our local team of community psychiatric nurses, all of whom work with the parents of our daily children. After considering all the implications we decided to run a pilot project. It seemed to work but adaptations were found to be necessary according to the needs of our children and also because we were initially using it in the classroom.

Our first revision introduced several more developmental stages and eliminated the 'Americanisms'. Subsequently, however, we went through every item. Mrs Mountain, our speech therapist, is responsible for the language checklist and this owes little to the original, other than format. Mrs Lee-Kelland, Educational Psychologist for the children who attend daily, re-wrote the cognitive checklist. The school staff took the remaining three checklists to alter and adapt as necessary. The extent of this revision can be gauged by the fact that less than two-thirds of our final socialization and motor checklist items are copied from the original. We re-organized the self-help checklist under seven headings, so that eating, drinking, washing and so forth could be considered separately. By so doing, we found that we needed to amend or add items to such an extent that the majority of this section is now of our own devising. We added a practical number skills section to the numeracy section, originally produced by Pond Meadow School, Guildford.

Each class uses Portage with modifications according to the needs of each child. The four special care classes comprise children from the Ellen Terry Home and several day children, the majority of whom have some visual defect. Thus it was necessary to adapt the largely visually based checklists to suit the needs of these young people.

Initial assessment of visual competence

It is an important fact that seventy-five per cent of children classified as 'blind' have residual sight. Therefore it is imperative, before using the Portage checklist, to assess how much the child can see or in fact wants to see. This involves not only motivation and experience but the degree and type of damage the child has suffered. This in turn will affect the way he or she makes use of functional vision in day-to-day activities.

Obviously, it is helpful for the assessor to know what aspect of the child's vision is most affected by the impairment.

If visual *acuity* is affected it means that an image is not clearly seen. Many factors can reduce acuity including retinal damage, refractive errors such as long or short sight, astigmatism, squint, even disuse, and levels of lighting.
If the problem lies in the child's *field of vision* the reception of visual images from different positions is affected. There are many different 'kinds' of loss of the visual field – patchy, restricted, tunnel, blind spots (loss of field in the same parts of both eyes).

Another area concerns *ocular skills*. These are the skills established in infancy which may be impaired or under-developed in the severely mentally handicapped child – for example, fixing focusing, converging the eyes, tracking, the transferring of focus from short to long, or to short distance and scanning.

Having established possible problem areas and attempted to assess the child's functional vision, it is important to act upon this knowledge immediately in relation to environment, materials and teaching objectives, bearing in mind that it is a continuous 'on-going' assessment.

Method of assessment

Observation is a continuous process and would ideally take place at those times when the child is engrossed in a task he or she finds motivating to such a degree that any vision he or she has is used to maximum effect. Mealtimes are frequently good opportunities, because even our most unmotivated youngsters find food rewarding, enabling us to observe:

a) whether they are visually curious, or show preference for handling, mouthing or sniffing

b) whether visual awareness of people is shown as the observer moves towards them

c) whether the child watches for his or her plate

d) whether the plate can be seen from the other side of the room or only when it is placed in front of him or her

e) the distance at which the child prefers to look at objects and people

f) the position of the object or person in relation to the child's visual field, from which angle and whether from the dominant side

g) the extent to which vision is used to direct and monitor the act of reaching and grasping

h) accuracy in both distance and direction when stretching the hand to grasp an object

i) how quickly something on the periphery of the visual field has been noticed

j) whether interest is affected by shape, colour, brightness, size or pattern

k) whether interest is directed to the object because other senses are more strongly attracted to it. For example, time and place are two variables that can affect visual response, as they may be related to comfort, competing stimuli, motivation and lighting.

Factors of constancy

Ideally four factors should, if possible, be constant – although all will change over a period of time. The first and most important of these is the assessor who needs to have built up a good relationship with the child and be able to interpret every nuance of the child's response. Second, the child in turn should be at his 'best', alert, clean and dry, not hungry or thirsty but warm and ready to participate in the learning game. Third, the room used for this assessment should be familiar and have the lighting placed correctly for the child and time of the year – seasonal change is an important consideration. Last, the stimulus used to attract the child's attention should have no competition that could divert his interest. Naturally this will be variable in colour, pattern, size, shape and additional sensory properties as well as in angle of presentation and distance to gain the child's awareness and interest.

Portage task presentation

With this assessment procedure in mind, although it is only superficial, we can begin to introduce Portage aiming thereby for some degree of independent purposeful behaviours. Also necessary is a modicum of communication, adequate use of the remaining senses and some self-help skills. To assist our task-presentation we occasionally use a 'blacklight lamp' as this helps to stimulate residual vision. It is also known as the ultra-violet light box. Basically it is a protected ultra-violet light under which it is possible to encourage children to make full use of limited vision and develop and improve hand-eye coordination, recognition of colour, size, shape, texture, near and distance, body image and some self-help skills. Activities denied in one way or another because of poor vision such as painting, drawing, modelling and board games can be participated in normally. Thus with adaptation and imagination the visual training techniques normally used under ordinary white light can be successfully used under black light. A frequent problem for some children is that they do not know how to 'see' because they have not built up the association and referral centres in the optic area of the brain and cannot therefore compare, accept or reject. Using an ultra-violet light with a carefully planned part of the Portage programme encourages the child to make full use of his or her impaired vision. The activity can then be continued in natural light once awareness is evident. It must, however, be emphasized that black light is not necessarily successful with every child. It is of course important to use fluorescent materials with the UVA. Ordinary colouring will not work because fluorescent colour saturation and brilliance is thirty times more visible than the same colour under normal white light.

Visual handicap/mental handicap

I have considered visual problems without referring to the children's other disabilities. All the children in the Ellen Terry Home are multiply handicapped. Much has been written on mental handicap and visual handicap but little which indicates how one affects the other,and the only relevant test of mental and motor development is the Reynell-Zinkin scale which assesses the child's level in terms of intellectual processes established, rather than skills acquired. The RNIB publish a small booklet,* *Guidelines for Teachers and Parents of Visually Handicapped Children with Additional Handicaps*. It raises several points and responds to some difficulties frequently encountered. However, one of our best aids is a 'Lilli Nielsen board', used primarily by our speech therapist, Mrs. Mountain. This is a platform which acts as a soundboard and is flexible with movement. Use of this, with an adapted Portage 'infant stimulation

---

*Available from RNIB, Gt. Portland St., London.

programme', has helped many of our most severely handicapped children to make startling progress. (Lilli Nielsen is a Child Welfare Consultant in a school for blind and partially sighted severely mentally handicapped children in Denmark.)

Portage, therefore, at Ellen Terry and Brooklands has not only been altered to suit our needs but has also supported and been used in conjunction with other aids and ideas. Consider, for example, two areas on the checklist: Self-help Skills and Language. The Self-help Skills, as previously mentioned, were divided into seven sections – Dressing, Undressing, Drinking, Feeding, Washing, Toileting and General skills. Isolating specific skill areas has made the organization of developmental progress easier to chart, and enabled staff to consider consecutive steps.

Dressing, for example, moves through twenty-seven steps on the checklist. These steps can, through the use of the Portage cards we have made, be further subdivided and monitored on activity charts. This section develops from 'Holds out arms and legs when being undressed' to 'Realizes the consequences of adding or removing clothes'. For the severely visually handicapped child, where appropriate, physical rather than imitative prompts are given. Similarly, the Language Section has been divided into two main areas dealing with Comprehension and Expressive language.

It should be evident, from the few examples given that we have modified some steps, added new ones and changed the format to cater for the child with an additional problem of visual handicap. I must add that our one little blue box has had to be extended to four in order to accommodate the extra cards we have devised.

Portage with Asian families in Central Birmingham

Janet Bardsley and Elizabeth Perkins

Janet Bardsley was formerly a Social Worker and Portage Adviser working with the Central Birmingham Portage Service. Elizabeth Perkins is District Psychologist and Portage Supervisor, South Birmingham Health Authority.

Summary

This paper presents information about Portage with families of Asian origin in Central Birmingham. Some of the findings of other workers will be described, data will be presented from the current service, and some suggestions will be made for others who are considering working with similar groups.

The Service

Central Birmingham Health Authority has a population of approximately 185,000. The area covered takes in Edgbaston and Harborne, two of the most prestigious and expensive places to live in Birmingham, and at the other end, Balsall Heath and Sparkbrook, both of which are in the area designated inner city. Birmingham Inner City Profile for 1982 shows that these areas are amongst the most deprived in the city. For example, they have almost the highest level of unemployment and the highest number of households without a bath and toilet. This area also has the highest proportion of new Commonwealth and Pakistan households. This is reflected in the fact that 11 of the 22 children so far referred to the Portage scheme have been of Asian origin.

The Portage service in Central Birmingham Health Authority was set up as a joint project between the Health Authority, initially just the clinical psychologist, and Barnardo's. Elizabeth Perkins and

Janet Bardsley planned the service and decided right from the start to attempt as far as possible to replicate the original Wessex Project, and to offer help to all clients referred regardless of race. The service was discussed with all relevant professionals, for example, paediatricians and speech therapists, most of whom agreed to help when necessary. It was not possible to assemble a management team, although both workers reported back through their own management structure, and it was arranged that the service would report annually to the Joint Care Planning Team for Mentally Handicapped People. Unfortunately, this team has since been disbanded and there is no District Handicap Team in Central Birmingham Health Authority.

Within a couple of months of the service beginning, an important development occurred. Other professionals in the District suggested setting up an informal group to coordinate services for pre-school children. The group now meets fortnightly to discuss all referrals of pre-school children and has representatives from all relevant professionals in Health, Social Services, Education and the voluntary sector. It has made the service run more smoothly and ensures that services are not missed or unnecessarily duplicated.

The procedure is that all families receive the same service. Every referral is taken to the pre-school liaison group and discussed. If there is agreement that the case should be taken on, professionals concerned with the child are contacted. The home adviser then makes an initial visit to the family and explains the service. If the family accepts, the service is started. An individual programme plan is drawn up on each child in consultation with the parents and other professionals. The project has one full-time home adviser and two part-timers both of whom are trained by the clinical psychologist. Supervision takes place once a week. The home advisers are positively monitored by the supervisor at six-monthly intervals for each child. A report is written on each child by the home adviser every six months.

Asian Parents and Portage

Parents receiving Portage have to be able to carry out certain procedures – for example, model the activity in front of the home adviser, put aside certain times of the day to teach the child, fill in activity charts and so on. How effectively a parent does this, and how much help the home adviser will need to give, will depend on the skills that the parents bring to Portage.

Boyd *et al.* (1977) say that these skills lie mainly in the areas of child management and teaching. The home adviser needs to assess sensitively how skilled the parents are in these areas in order to provide effective instruction. Although they admit that a suitable assessment procedure for these skills does not exist, they hope that the Portage Parent Programme will provide an approximation to these goals.

Half the families involved in the Birmingham Portage Service are of Asian origin. There were doubts expressed by a variety of other professionals about the ability of Asian families to use Portage, including predictions that economic, language and cultural barriers would make Portage less effective with them.

In the study done by Perkins and Powell (1983) there was an attempt to clarify these issues. Four prerequisite skills for Portage were hypothesized and an interview study of eleven Asian families with a pre-school handicapped child was carried out to see if the families possessed them. The skills were:

1. Belief in child development: having the idea that children develop skills in an orderly sequence which is more or less the same for all children.
2. Belief in teaching: believing that a child's development can be accelerated by intervention and that parents have an important contribution to make to this.
3. Knowledge of handicap and its implications: realising that the child has problems in learning as well as in other areas; understanding that something can be done, and that the child can learn, but also having an appreciation of the child's limitations.
4. Opportunities for teaching: accepting that changing the environment, including their own behaviour, can help the child learn.

Some of the findings were as follows.

1. Belief in child development. Most families were able to state milestones of development although, interestingly, on skills that are mainly motor dependent such as sitting and walking the stated ages were similar to Western norms, whereas with those more dependent on learning such as washing and dressing the ages given were different from Western norms.

2. Belief in teaching. The answers here were mixed, depending on what needed to be taught. For example, most families felt that children could be taught to walk, but few felt they could be taught to be dry by day.
3. Knowledge of Handicap. Of the families studied seven had no idea of what was wrong with their children and the implications of their handicaps.
4. Opportunities for teaching. The families studied had few commercial toys, and rarely played with the children as we in Western cultures term play.

The evidence seems to be that many of these families may not have all the hypothesized prerequisite skills for Portage. The questions that need to be answered are: are they in fact prerequisite skills? Can the family carry out the essentials without them? Do we in fact need to look more closely at different skills and utilize these?

Data from Central Birmingham Portage Service

A Portage Service necessarily accumulates records on all clients. After one year of operating, data from Central Birmingham Portage Service have enabled the authors to compare Asian and English families on a variety of parameters to examine how far Asian families have been able to carry out Portage procedures, compared with English families.

After a year of the service 22 children have been referred, and two have not been followed up because other people have been involved with them. Eleven of the children have been Asian, and 11 English. The youngest was eight months old when referred, and the oldest four years. No parent has refused the service; that is, asked the home adviser not to visit or been consistently out at the arranged time without explanation.

Further data on the children are presented in Tables 1 to 4. From these it can be seen that there was no apparent difference between Asian and English families in the number of activity charts set, the number returned and the number of goals achieved. The English families raised slightly more problems about other issues than did the Asian families.

Differences in Portage practice between Asian and English families

The operation of a Portage Service to Asian and English clients has revealed qualitative differences between the two groups which are not measured by the data so far presented. These differences are the subjective impressions of the authors, although substantiated to some extent by other workers. They are noted in order to:

1. help prepare and inform people planning to do Portage with Asian families,
2. help people move towards and clarify more sensitive measures of the quality of Portage Service to all people receiving it, and
3. illustrate that the 'cultural' differences white professionals might perceive when doing Portage with Asian families do not interfere with the parents' ability to achieve weekly goal setting, daily teaching and record keeping with their children.

Family life

Roles in Asian families tend to be fairly well circumscribed, although they will vary according to the family's religion, place of origin, and so on. For example, Ghuman (1975), described the background of people who have emigrated from the Indian Punjab. He says that the roles of men and women in such families are clearly separated and strongly adhered to. He has done a small study looking at Indian Punjabis living in Nottingham and has found little change in these roles. It is important to know about what roles are taken by family members, particularly the women, as Portage tends to concentrate on the mother. Of the eleven Asian families visited in the Birmingham Portage Service, work with one family is with a father. Otherwise with all families, English or Asian, work is with the mothers. Having children, for some Asian families, may have a different emphasis from that placed on it by most English families. Families can be large and although the women find child rearing care hard work, many feel four to five children a respectable target for their nuclear family. It means that, because of cultural attitudes in which the whole family, rather than the women in isolation, takes responsibility, rarely are the home adviser and mother/father alone with the child. There are invariably other brothers, sisters, cousins, aunts, uncles and grandparents to join in the teaching. There is often a cultural significance for families in having a boy in the family. It can even be more significant than the fact that the child is handicapped, and families sometimes continue to have children despite advice that the handicap will arise again. Two of the families visited have more than one handicapped child in the family. For one family two children are receiving the Portage Service.

Language

All the Asian families receiving Portage are Moslems from North Pakistan or Bangladesh and speak Punjabi, Urdu or Bengali. This is characteristic of the Asian people living in Central Birmingham. Only one of the mothers speaks English. These observations are similar to the findings of Dutt and DaCunha (1982). They studied twenty Asian families in part of Birmingham's inner city and found that only two of the women concerned spoke English. This has meant that to all families but one the Portage Service has been delivered through an interpreter. The interpreters are given two hours' training before they work with the service and it is checked that the interpreter speaks the same language as the family. All the interpreters except one have young children themselves. Meetings are held for the interpreters to discuss the visits, to do role plays, and check the use of words. It needs to be remembered, however, that working through a third person is both more long-winded and less sensitive than direct contact. Messages can get lost both ways. The skills of the home adviser as well as the interpreter have to be developed, both to convey messages and to check on what the parent is saying.

In the eleven families only one of the mothers reads English. However, activity charts written in English are left and efforts are made to ensure that the parents are recording their teaching. An attempt has been made to deliver the same service to everyone and thus it was not considered appropriate to miss out a key variable such as the activity chart. Additionally, and perhaps most importantly, the writing and the collecting of activity charts helps control the home advisers in that they have to set teaching targets and ways of measuring them. Activity charts also help to make it clear to all parents that they are attempting to teach specific skills to their children.

Child rearing practices and play

The service has found some differences in child rearing practices and play amongst Asian families. This supports the findings of other workers. Ghuman (1975), Henly (1979), Davenport (1983) have pointed out that Asian children in Asia or in England are brought up in a relatively 'permissive' way in the sense that many are fed on demand, sleep when they feel like it and are generally given a lot of attention from the extended family. They have few commercial toys and tend to interact with peers rather than with adults. Davenport points out that Asian children, because of the way they are brought up, tend to learn about the world more through observation and doing than through playing at doing. Her study was done in Smethwick and Ghuman's in Nottingham. In the study previously mentioned, Perkins and Powell (1983) interviewed eleven Asian families in West Birmingham, and found that only four of the mothers interviewed said they played with their child. Ten of the children had toys but they tended to be soft toys and picture books.

In Birmingham the experience with the Portage Service has been not only that there is a lack of commercial toys, but also that there are less obvious materials available in the home to play with. Characteristically, the houses visited are simply furnished. The sitting rooms usually have two or three settees and a television on a shelf high on the wall. They appear to be designed primarily for adult conversation and entertaining, not particularly to occupy a pre-school child. The families worked with are poor but also have different financial priorities, for example, supporting families back in Pakistan, and they do not see buying commercial toys as a reasonable way of spending money. When asked, they mostly state that they never had toys themselves and describe a life style where as children they were outside playing with cousins and siblings and learning practical skills with their parents. The toys that are seen and available in local shops are cheap, dangerous and easily broken (Galt's have not yet got an outlet in Balsall Heath or Sparkbrook) and there appears to be little understanding or appreciation that toys can be a way of stimulating children to acquire new skills.

There are some guidelines that can be used for a Portage Service applied to Asian families.

1. If teaching that involves equipment needs to be done it has to be taken in to the home.

2. Toys that are left will be attractive to the other children in the house and get dismantled or lost by them, possibly

leaving the handicapped child without the necessary materials.

3. It is possible to make toys from junk materials so that parents can see that yoghurt pots and cotton reels are as good to give the child to play with as anything.

An aspect of doing Portage with Asian families, which does seem to be significantly different from Portage with English families, is the difference in routines. Portage as a package seems to be very much set in the culture of mid-west America, and in the package there is a model of a child with special child equipment and special child routines. In the Asian families visited there is a different model of routines. There is a different style of life that does not consist of the more routine/controlled/orderly style, implicit in the Portage materials. These differences need to be taken into account when activities are set so that they fit into the child's and family's life style.

Reactions to handicap

The Asian families seemed to react differently to their child's handicap than the English families did. For example, they seem to find it harder to grasp that there is no *medical* intervention that will cure their child. The illusion that the medical profession can magically remove all ills is not a phenomenon exclusive to Asian parents of handicapped children; however, half of the Asian families have asked about medical advice. These questions include 'Where can we get a doctor?' 'Why can't our child have an operation?' 'If the doctors can now cure typhoid, why can't they cure our child?' No English family visited by the Portage Service has asked such questions or sought this kind of advice. This may be because English families have had more exposure to the Health Service. Related to this is the observation that none of the Asian parents with profoundly handicapped children (four families) that are visited seemed to celebrate the success their child has and they may not accept approximations to the required target behaviour. For example, the mother of a child with athetoid movements did not count her child's jerky attempts to grasp an object as a success. Another family with a child with extremely floppy movements did not count her efforts at 'lifting head for ten seconds when placed in corner seat' as a success because she could not do it for ten minutes, even though there was accurate recording and teaching of activities. Conversely, the English families visited are more able to report and enthuse about new things their children have done and changes in behaviour in their similarly profoundly handicapped children. It is probable that we need to secure more Portage visitors from the same cultural background in order to explain things more clearly.

Conclusion

The evidence from Birmingham is that an effective Portage Service can be delivered to Asian families as to English families. There are, however, qualitative differences in the operation of the service to the two groups which require much more understanding of the advantages as well as the disadvantages of differing cultural attitudes. Any worker going into the homes of Asian families needs to be sensitive to the possible differences in priorities, attitudes and ideas another culture might have. Nevertheless, the service in Central Birmingham has demonstrated that Asian families can teach their handicapped children various skills using Portage methods.

Table 1: No. of visits per week where activity charts were set over a two-month period

Week starting	*Asian*	*English*
16.5.83	*5/7	7/8
23.5.83	6/7	5/8
30.5.83	3/7	3/8
6.6.83	7/7	7/8
13.6.83	6/7	8/8
20.6.83	5/7	7/7
27.6.83	4/6	7/8
4.7.83	3/6	7/8
11.7.83	4/6	6/8

* The denominator is the number of visits that week, and the numerator is the number of visits where activity charts were set.

Table 2: Ratio of activity charts returned to activity charts set for the first 14 children receiving the service

	Asian		*English*
Child 1	29/30	Child 8	19/30
2	0/5	9	8/8
3	13/13	10	13/29
4	3/4	11	7/12
5	6/16	12	26/26
6	10/11	13	14/23
7	5/12	14	35/38

Table 3: Ratio of goals achieved to goals set for the first 14 children to receive the service. (Taken from post-baseline measure on activity chart and record of home visit).

	Asian		*English*
Child 1	24/36	Child 8	21/30
2	3/5	9	8/8
3	10/13	10	13/29
4	3/4	11	9/12
5	10/16	12	23/26
6	7/10	13	13/23
7	5/12	14	20/28

Table 4: Other problems raised by the first 14 families to receive the service

	Asian	*English*
Financial	3	3
Housing	2	0
Other Agency	3	7
Equipment	4	4
English	1	0
Family (other children)	0	4
	13	18

Help requested and noted on home visiting record and discussed at supervision.

An Intervention Package to Teach Parents of Severely Retarded and Severely Non-compliant Children and Adults at Home to Teach Their Child New Relevant Skills

Albert Kushlick, John Smith, Alison Gold

Health Care Evaluation Research Team

Introduction

There is good and rapidly growing evidence that the Portage Home Teaching intervention enables home visitors from different educational and professional backgrounds to train most parents with severely mentally handicapped children to teach their children new skills (Shearer and Shearer, 1972; Schortinghuis and Frohman, 1974; Smith *et al*, 1977; Revill and Blunden, 1979). Training is observed to take place under the following conditions:

— in their own homes
— in the presence of the home teacher

and there is evidence that teaching also goes on when the parent is on her or his own. So far there is no observational evidence to show that parents generalize their newly learned systematic teaching skills to other settings such as other locations in the home, at school, work or in leisure settings, or to other conditions, such as different times of the day or night, or in the presence of friends, neighbours, relatives and other professionals.

There is also evidence that a minority of those receiving Portage teaching (Bluma *et al.*, 1976) do not respond to the intervention, particularly those clients with severe orthopaedic and neurological deficits, and physically able people with severe communication and compliance deficits, even in the presence of a trained Portage home teacher or supervisor (Smith *et al.*, op. cit.; Felce *et al.*, in press). However, since the early 1970's, evidence has been accumulating to show that parents or teachers of physically able non-complying children and adults can be taught by specialist teachers to follow a rigorously defined teaching interaction, with precise criteria for the delivery of instructions, prompts and consequences. Children and adults make gains in these settings which are related functionally (Lovaas *et al.*, 1967, Koegel *et al.*, 1977 and 1980) to the teaching procedures followed.

There are no replications by non-specialist service personnel of similar successes with these procedures. More important, there has been no description of these procedures in manual form so that they can be successfully replicated and delivered by inservice-trained visiting professionals as part of a standard domiciliary service to families with severely mentally retarded children and adults living at home. Finally, there has been no description of service interventions which successfully teach parents of non-complying, severely retarded children and adults to follow the teaching interactions with very high degrees of precision in formal settings, let alone in settings within and outside the home, and under the key conditions presenting problems to the families. If children and adults with very severe communication, compliance and attention deficits are both to acquire and generalize new skills, it seems likely that many thousands of precise teaching trials are required under a very wide range of conditions.

We believe that it is useful to consider the following steps separately in relation to attaining these targets.

Step 1 Parents should be taught to implement the precision teaching interaction in a single formal teaching setting. They should know how to a) get the child's attention and b) arrange for the child to follow an instruction and experience effective consequences for learning, both in the presence of professionals and when professionals are not present.

Step 2 **They should then be taught how to implement this interaction in a range of key *informal* settings, both in the presence of the professionals and when they are not present.**

Step 3 It should be arranged that parents maintain the above-mentioned skills on their own in new formal and informal settings.

Our approach to this task includes developing methods of helping parents to deal effectively and robustly with emotional discomfort encountered during the intervention. This involves shaping parental verbal (cognitive) and emotional behaviour as parents describe with increasing precision their current parenting skills, and as they evaluate their skills and their experiences in practising the new skills through their successes and failures in implementing the new procedures in a range of settings under different conditions. If successful, these steps end with a firm public commitment by parents to attain agreed objectives with specified procedures. This paper presents some preliminary findings from our DHSS-funded research.

The research aims to develop a set of procedures which can be used by professionals to teach staff visiting the homes of severely retarded children and adults with major difficulties in communication to instruct the parent in implementing a precise teaching interaction similar to those described by Lovaas *et al.* (1980) and Koegel *et al.* (1980) in any setting under all conditions. It is our aim that the parents will, after experiencing initial emotional discomfort and pessimism, do this with calm, confidence and optimistic interest. When, as is likely, emotional discomfort and pessimism return, they will be able to detect its cognitive source, take steps to confront it and to continue with the programme.

Subjects and settings

Over a period of two years we plan to intervene with families in the Southampton or Winchester areas. These families will have been referred to us because professionals in contact with them consider that the families are having significant problems teaching their children new skills because of severe non-compliance which may also be disruptive, destructive or assaultive. We will not include handicapped persons with additional orthopaedic or sensory deficits in this grant period.

This paper deals with our first two families. One subject, who came from Winchester, was four years old when the study began and had previously received Portage home teaching; the other was a thirty-five year-old adult.

This study is initially concerned with shaping the performance of the parents of these mentally handicapped people so that they give a single, clear, instruction, wait, prompt when necessary and respond to the behaviour in the way advocated by Lovaas *et al.* (1980) and Koegel *et al.* (1977). Later, this training will be extended to include professionals, such as teachers or community nurses who are in frequent contact with the handicapped person. Changes in the compliance of the handicapped person will be monitored as a function of the parent training (Kushlick and Smith, 1982).

At the outset, the first handicapped subject was four and attended the local nursery school on three days per week and an opportunity playgroup on two days per week. He had a hearing deficit in one ear and was given a hearing aid which he wore irregularly and when he chose to. He had a wide range of motor skills and an expressive vocabulary vocally, and in Makaton, signs of about twenty words. His receptive vocabulary was wider. At the time we began our study, he complied with about one request in ten in the course of mealtimes, and when bathing and dressing at home. He spent much of his time engaged with materials on his own, but seldom responded to requests from adults to use any of these materials. He sometimes played inappropriately, despite repeated requests not to, with breakable and possibly dangerous materials like electric lamps. He was able to feed himself with his fingers or a spoon. He was able to cooperate with an adult washing or dressing him when he chose to do so. He played in parallel with his two-year-old brother who was developing normally and with the children at the nursery school. His parents arranged his routines of getting up, toileting, dressing, eating, bathing and preparation for bed so that each activity was done together with his younger brother. His parents were in their late twenties and pursued career activities very keenly. They shared child care activities and arranged for paid child carers at home while they both worked outside and at home as artists and art teachers. The child was referred by the teachers at the nursery school because they predicted more difficult problems would arise if the non-complying behaviour continued or increased as the boy grew older.

The second handicapped person was thirty-five, and attended the Southampton Social Education Centre (SEC) about one day in every two or three weeks. He had a wide range of motor skills despite his club foot. He also had a wide range of receptive language skills but, despite his facial expressions and vocal language topographies, very few of his words were used meaningfully. He complied on first request with about one out of five requests from his father and about one in two requests from his mother. He was referred to us by the SEC staff because he very frequently failed to attend the Centre, and because his parents reported that he behaved violently towards them when they tried to get him up in the morning, or to switch off his television late at night. He spent over ninety per cent of his time at home in his bedroom – most of his waking time was spent watching television and he had all of his meals in his bedroom lying down in his bed. He was able to feed himself but was completely washed and dressed, usually by his mother. His violent outbursts occurred infrequently – he threw cushions at the television and trinkets downstairs, hit out and kicked out mainly at his mother. Three outbursts (one per day for three days consecutively) took place over a period of eight months while we were visiting. His father had been a skilled boatbuilder but had recently retired after a few years of unemployment. He had a severe hearing defect caused by bomb blast in the Second World War which led to a speech defect, so that he was intelligible only with difficulty. He was unable to participate at all in our early family interviews. The mother was a pensioner who had never worked outside the home. They had a grown-up son who lived at home and a married son and daughter who lived nearby. Both parents were concerned about their son.

Method

Once a family has been referred to us, oriented to our approach, and has agreed to collaborate, we have developed the following procedures for implementation during subsequent visits to the family home.

i) Interview to elicit a detailed account of what the parents *want* the handicapped person to do from the time he/she gets up to the time he/she goes to sleep, and how this compares with the current performance. This covers all locations in the house and outside. At the end of these interviews we arrive at a statement of the outcomes desired by parents. We check this statement with the families and leave them tape recordings of the interview to re-evaluate it before we arrive at our final statement of outcomes.

ii) Interview/direct observation to assess the handicapped person's current repertoire on the Portage Checklist, supplemented by the Bender *et al.* checklist (1976) and the Wessex Revised Portage Language Checklist (1983). We also use this to check the family preferences of new skills they would like to teach the handicapped person.

iii) Following permission we take video films of:
  a) the family's 'best' time with the handicapped person,
  b) the family's 'worst' time with the handicapped person,
  c) the parents giving the handicapped person sixteen specific instructions to carry out tasks which our data show are currently in the repertoire of the handicapped person.

iv) We analyse the effectiveness of the parent-child teaching interaction recorded on the video film.
i.e. parental – Instructions (S^D)
– Prompts
– Consequences (S^R)
} during both structured and unstructured teaching

At the same time we categorize the response of the handicapped person in relation to these instructions as

C	complied without help
C	complied with help
E	engaged
N	neutral no instruction given
NC	non-compliance
D	disruptive non-compliance

v) We demonstrate our complete acceptance of the family and handicapped person by telling the parents that what they are doing is as it should be now, evidence being that it has delivered results so far. We then feed back the results of the videotaping. This is used firstly as a 'fun' television show, and secondly as a systematic demonstration that teaching and learning could be different if the parents chose to make it so. It is pointed out to the parents how their current teaching compares with an option we believe to be more effective and efficient.

vi) We respond to parental comments on the feedback, shaping up their precision of description and evaluation as we do so.

vii) We demonstrate a model of a more effective teaching interaction:
  a) we show a videotape of the research team members roleplaying Step 1 of a basic teaching interaction (see (ix) below)

b) we show part of a videotape of Lovaas *et al.* teaching skills (Lovaas and Burton Leat, 1981) to developmentally delayed children. This gives a forward-looking picture of how things might be with alternative methods of teaching.

viii) We respond to parental comments on these films and check whether parents accept these as useful models.

ix) Where parents agree to work for these new outcomes, we teach them to roleplay our Step 1. This is a teaching interaction which contains the basic components to elicit correct responses to the instructions 'sit down', 'look at me' and 'stand up'. We later include the basic corrections (verbal and non-verbal) 'sit up straight' and 'hands quiet'. Parents roleplay Step 1 with us and with one another until they attain a sufficiently high degree of precision to practice on their own. We video their efforts and play them back to them immediately, highlighting and celebrating successes, and pointing out areas in need of improvement.

x) We request that parents practise Step 1 of roleplay with one another as homework, keeping records of doing so, and keeping an audiotape on during the practice.

xi) When parents have reached criterion on Step 1 roleplay, we request them to give sixteen instructions to the handicapped person and video them doing so as a baseline. The sixteen instructions are selected from tasks which the handicapped person is known to be able to carry out. We play this film back to the parents and we point out the deficits and excesses it contains. We also show the parents videotapes of our alternative roleplaying of selected instructions taken from the sixteen they gave. These incorporate the procedures they have learned in Step 1 roleplay. If they agree with our alternatives, we then teach them Step 2 which is giving these instructions in a standard, structured setting. We ask them to practise these daily until they reach criterion.*

xii) Together with the parents, we set long-term goals to be negotiated with the other visiting professionals.

---

*At the time of presenting this paper, we had reached this stage only with the five-year-old boy.

xiii) At this stage, we arrange a meeting with all professionals involved with the family including those who referred the family. We demonstrate at this meeting how we have been working. The parents are able to report directly to this meeting and to check that the professionals agree with the aims of the proposed intervention before the parents begin working directly with the handicapped person.

xiv) We arrange for the parents to begin working directly with the handicapped person at home on the first step of each of the long-term goals agreed at the meeting with the professionals.

We have now systemised these steps out of our earlier valuable experiences and setbacks and will follow them in this order on new cases. The actual steps taken in the cases reported were slightly different.

Results: family 1

The video recordings of this family showed:

(i) FIRST BASELINE FILM OF BATHING AND DRESSING IN PYJAMAS BEFORE BED

In relation to each task carried out by their son (B), both the father and mother gave him many instructions. In nearly all of these, they neither waited until the child was quiet, nor did they attract his attention (e.g. get eye contact) before giving him an instruction. The instructions were often not clear nor systematic. B seldom followed the instructions and the parents then repeated the instructions up to five or six times. On very few occasions did they follow up B's non-complying behaviour by physically prompting him through the required task. When his parents did prompt the response physically, they also repeated the instructions verbally. When B responded correctly to an instruction or to a physical prompt, he was seldom given a clearly observable and audible positive reinforcer.

(ii) At first getting dressed time and at first dinner-time, the video record showed the same features.

(iii) At later sessions at night at their home, the parents received instructions on roleplaying parent-child interactions. These involved, in Step 1, getting B to sit down, stand up and make eye contact on request. Over a period of several weeks of practising the roleplayed procedures with guidance and with video feedback, the parents transformed their performance under formal teaching conditions:

- they ensured that the person playing B was not behaving disruptively before giving 'him' any instruction
- similarly, they ensured that 'he' made eye contact with them on request before they gave 'him' further instructions
- they gave 'him' clear, positive reinforcers when 'he' successfully carried out a request with or without help
- they presented 'him' with clear, negative reinforcers (corrections modelled by the researchers to be followed by the parents) when 'he' failed to follow the instructions or behaved non-compliantly or disruptively.

These roleplay sessions took place approximately once per week for about one hour in the evening at the parents' home. The participants were initially a parent working with one researcher while the other researcher took the video films. Subsequently both parents worked together while one researcher filmed and the other gave feedback to the parent. Still later, feedback was not given during the practice. It was given after the practice was completed using film showed on the video monitor.

During the course of the roleplay practices, the parents said that they had unilaterally begun implementing the newly-learned procedures directly with B. They claimed that they had done so successfully and that no further practice trials were needed. Despite the evidence of successful instructions, prompts and delivery of consequences in roleplay, repeat baseline films of bathing and mealtimes showed that there was no change from the parental interactions at the original baseline.

The parents then listed sixteen tasks which B was known to carry out on request. The researchers filmed B's mother giving these instructions to B before she had been instructed on how to apply the procedures practised in roleplays. This film showed that the problem continued; that is when working directly with B, she gave B instructions before he had been quiet for five seconds, and when he was not attending to her. She repeated instructions and changed them when B failed to respond to them. She failed to prompt B physically to carry out the tasks when he failed to respond for over five seconds, or did something other than the task instructed within five seconds.

Both parents agreed that it would be helpful to practise giving B the additional instructions through roleplay before working directly with B. These training sessions were then started.

During a two-hour interview on 4th October 1983 with both parents, we checked the extent to which they accepted the nature of the problem and targets as we described them. We also checked with them some key implications of this acceptance for working systematically to implement the procedures. At the end of this interview, the parents agreed to practise Step 1 of the roleplay procedures daily. These were carried out for between ten and thirty minutes during evening meetings held at their home. Video feedback was given after each filming. After the sixteen instructions had been filmed with the mother, they were also shown the videotape of these. Examples of an alternative interaction based on the Step 1 procedures, roleplayed by AG and AK, were shown. They agreed to practise this form of Step 1 of the roleplay procedures at supervised meetings at their home and on their own. When they had attained criterion at Step 1 procedures, they were shown an alternative of Step 2 – that is, using the Step 1 procedures when giving some of the sixteen instructions modelled by the researchers and demonstrated on video and *in vivo* in their home. The parents agreed to practise these and the mother did so with researchers supervising and giving feedback.

Results: family 2

In evolving these steps, we believe we made errors of haste in relation to one of the first two families. At the time of writing, the parents of the thirty-five-year-old severely developmentally delayed man had followed some of these steps in relation to their son. They began roleplaying Step 1 immediately after observing some trials by members of the research team (AK and JS). After roleplaying in the lounge and dining room in our presence, they asked to and began instructing their son directly under these conditions, that is, before any meeting had been called to discuss progress and future proposals with the professionals already concerned with the family.

The video-recordings of this family showed:

(i) FIRST BASELINE FILM OF GETTING UP IN THE MORNING, WASHING, TOILETING, DRESSING AND BREAKFAST

The father brought N a cup of coffee and woke him up shortly after seven a.m. with a barely audible and indistinct request to wake up. When N turned over and continued to lie in bed with the blankets drawn up over his head, the father sighed and left the room, leaving N the coffee. He returned about thirty minutes later and repeated this. When N again failed to sit up or to emerge from under the bedclothes, Mr O repeated his instructions several times interspersed with sighs and shoulder shrugs. Fifteen minutes later, Mrs O entered and greeted N who responded by sitting up in bed and drinking his coffee.

Mrs O chatted to N about his clothes. When N made a verbal comment which was not comprehensible to us*, Mrs O engaged N by telling him what picture was on his wall, what programme was on the television that night and so on. N might interrupt Mrs O to ask if a named TV personality or trainer from his Social Education Centre would be around that day. Mrs O would reply as accurately as possible while tidying the room.

Mrs O began instructing N to get up out of bed, to put on his dressing gown and slippers. Despite Mrs O's failure to get N's attention, N complied with most requests after the first or second request. Most of Mrs O's requests were very clear and audible.

Mrs O often prompted N physically to complete an instructed task within five seconds of having given the instruction, i.e., before N had a clear opportunity to fail to implement it. Virtually all of Mrs O's physical prompts accompanied her instructions and ended in N's effectively carrying out the tasks requested of him. She gave very few clearly observable possible reinforcers when N successfully complied with instructions.

N maintained a continuing but largely meaningless chatter with Mrs O while she physically prompted him through undressing in the toilet, washing by hand, toileting, drying and re-dressing him in pyjamas. This

---

*These comments were repeated and incomprehensible. They included naming TV personalities and member of the Social Education Centre.

continued while she guided him physically through dressing in his bedroom. N appeared to take no initiatives except in sitting down, drinking coffee and asking repetitively if there was football or boxing on the television. Mrs O answered these questions repeatedly.

Mr O shaved N while he sat still on a chair, N took himself to the downstairs toilet, undressed sitting down, dressed and returned to the dining room where he sat until his taxi arrived.

He was physically prompted into his anorak and walked with help to the taxi.

(ii) INSTRUCTIONS BASELINE

The parents were asked while being filmed to give N instructions to carry out tasks which he was known to be able to carry out. The video-record showed that N followed about fifty per cent of Mrs O's instructions on first request. When N did not follow, Mrs O repeated the instruction at intervals of about two or three seconds until N carried them out. She gave few physical prompts or positive reinforcers when N successfully completed a task. She gave virtually no corrections when N failed to respond or responded non-compliantly by embracing Mrs O, putting his head on her shoulder and laughing.

(iii) Mr and Mrs O began roleplaying Step 1 – 'sit down', 'stand up', 'look at me', 'hands quiet', 'sit up straight' – and Step 2 instructions – 'show me your nose (knees, toes)', 'hands up', 'hands down', – with the researchers and then with one another. These activities were filmed by researchers or parents. They were fed back to the parents immediately afterwards. The activities took place in the parents' home during the day.

At their request, the parents began working directly with N while being given immediate feedback from the researchers. The parents asked to begin working with N directly on their own. The researchers agreed to this* before

---

*Under our current procedures, parents would not work directly with the handicapped person until they had demonstreated their ability to roleplay the procedures at criterion to all of the professionals involved, had set long-term goals and had attained support of all professionals involved with the family for the goals and the methods of working directly with the client.

further discussions with other professionals. The O's worked with N on their own and in the presence of the researchers.

Six days after the roleplay and direct intervention with their son had occurred, he had three episodes in which he behaved disruptively at home. He kicked out and hit at his parents (mainly his mother) and threw objects in the lounge and bedroom on the floor. Outbursts similar to those had occurred before our intervention, and were one of the criteria for our selecting this case. The general practitioner was called in by the parents. He gave tranquillisers ('Chlorpromazine') and called in the consultant in mental handicap from the local traditional hospital. He arranged for the transfer of the man to the traditional hospital 'for investigation'. The consultant told the family and GP that the outbursts were due to the stress of our invervention, and warned them not to continue working with the researchers and not to carry out the teaching procedures. The mother asked us not to continue and maintained this position when her son returned home from hospital. She continued to be friendly and gave us full permission to use the material assembled up to that point.

Discussion

The attainment by both families of a highly competent, technically complex teaching interaction and handicapped person compliance response after a very short roleplay interaction in the home is encouraging. We are now working on systematic interventions which will reduce the time taken for the parents to accept our definition of the problem, to discuss targets with the research team and to agree to use the intervention to attain these targets.

The delays which arose in relation to B's family related to:

i) practising, in the absence of the researchers, the skills practised in their presence

ii) keeping or continuing to maintain written records of their activities with the handicapped person

iii) keeping appointments to discuss their successes, and the future objectives or problems, i.e., obstacles to attaining their goals

iv) implementing the teaching interaction under the conditions of the handicapped person a) whining, crying or repeatedly walking away from the activity or b) behaving assaultively (hitting, kicking, head butting), or noisily (shouting), or looking angrily (angry eyes), i.e., the parents extinguishing the handicapped person's emotional and behavioural non-compliance and escape reactions to formal teaching.

Arising out of this experience we are also systemising our steps to attain the following.

i) Practising and mastering the new skills in other settings – other rooms in the house, the school or SEC, outside the house, and under other conditions in which the skills will be practised (e.g., with other people present such as friends, neighbours, relations, other professionals).

ii) Being available to explore problems of assaultiveness and other disturbed behaviours with the support of the researchers *before* requesting medical, eliminative or pathological interventions – drugs and transfer of the handicapped person to hospital.

The target of maintaining and generalising the new teaching interaction in specific settings in the absence of the intervening professionals is a key pre-requisite step to their being able to do so in all locations and under most conditions. The need to programme specifically for maintenance and generalization is now recognized (Stokes and Baer, 1977; Koegel *et al.*, 1978). Indeed, the difference between effective service interventions and 'pure' experimental interventions is that in the former, meaningful targets are maintained and generalized through interventions appropriate to attain these under a wide variety of conditions in the natural environment; in pure experimental interventions, success is said to be attained if changes are demonstrable only under very limited and specific laboratory conditions.

There is a range of possible independent variables or stimulus events – the roleplay procedures, verbal commitment to the value of the targets and the value of the procedures, various forms of monitoring and feedback. There are also likely to be influences from the order in which the components of the independent variable package are presented. We have not demonstrated a functional relationship between these and the dependent variable – the complex target of parents interacting effectively with the handicapped person in structured and unstructured settings. The video playback cannot function directly as a reinforcer of parental teaching behaviour because it occurs too long after teaching itself has stopped. It may function, together with other information given, as a rule which, if followed, will attain positive and avoid negative consequences (Skinner, 1969; Zettle and Hayes, 1980).

Whenever obstacles and 'failures' or criticisms arise in relation to the intervention, we are aware of our own and of the parents' negative, pessimistic verbal expressions and feelings in relation to the tasks as perceived and evaluated. We also note the extent to which these negative thoughts and feelings are sometimes accompanied by escape and avoidance behaviours. In maintaining our own efforts, we note the value of:

i) accepting and living with the possiblilty that the long-term generalisation targets may never be attained

ii) noting that this is not a tragedy but merely a frustrating situation which requires further exploration of the variables involved

iii) accepting that hundreds of thousands of imperfect trials have preceded our intervention and a similarly large number which are more effective may well be needed to attain generalization of appropriate skills in new settings.

We have also found it valuable to counter inaccurate and therefore irrational negative thoughts with accurate rational alternatives, and to act upon these counters in maintaining and generalizing our own behaviour under difficult conditions where we are strongly tempted to give up, or to procrastinate. We are therefore developing an intervention package based on the procedures of cognitive behaviour modification, rational emotive therapy and rational behaviour therapy (Beck, 1976; Meichanbaum, 1974; Ellis, 1962; Maultsby, 1975 and 1984) to assist parents and professionals to persist in their attempts to change important variables controlling effective implementation of the teaching interaction under all conditions, e.g., under conditions of non-compliance, whining and assaultive behaviour of the handicapped person, and of criticisms from relatives and other professionals.

We are particularly concerned to teach parents and professionals how to detect their thoughts and beliefs which evaluate situations (and especially people) negatively, and which are accompanied by intense negative feelings and actions which accompany them. According to Ellis (op. cit), the three major inaccurate beliefs are:

'I must be perfect'
'Others must be perfect in relation to me'
'The world must be perfect'.

The major inaccurate evaluations which arise in relation to these beliefs when events are perceived as *not* perfect are:

'I/others/the world are worthless or deserving of condemnation'
'It is terrible, awful, catastrophic that I/others/the world are not perfect'
'I/others/the world are hopeless and deserve punishment'
'I should not have to put up with the imperfections or discomfort'
'I can't stand it'

More specific feelings may arise from common combinations of beliefs and evaluations, for example:

Depression: 'I should be perfect'
'I am a bad/inferior person'
'This is awful'
'Poor me'
'I should not have this pain'
'I can't stand it'
'Poor others'
'They should not have this pain'
'It is hopeless – there is nothing anyone can do about it'

Anxiety: 'It will be awful if . . .'
'I will not be able to cope'
'I won't be able to stand it'
'It should not be awful'
'I should be able to predict the future and to cope'

Anger: 'How can you do that!'
'I can't stand it'
'You should be perfect'
'You are a bad/inferior person deserving punishment'

Guilt: 'How could I do that!'
'I should be perfect'
'I should not have done . . .'
'I am a bad/inferior person'
'I deserve punishment'.

Beck (op. cit.) has described specific categories of faulty thinking associated with depression and anxiety:

arbitrary and incorrect inferences: 'My friend/colleague/social worker has criticized me, therefore he thinks I'm a bad friend/parent/worker/client'

selective abstraction: 'He has asked me to keep records of my activities because he thinks I'm a liar'

over-generalization: 'My child does not do what I ask and therefore I am a bad parent'

magnification or catastrophization: 'If I treat my handicapped child differently from his brother, he will be stigmatized and excluded from school and his brother will become insanely jealous'

inexact labelling: 'If I follow precision teaching with my handicapped child, I will cease to be his mother'

Ellis and Harper (1975) have identified a number of widely held irrational beliefs which accompany negative emotions and interfere with the new learning and creative skills of people holding and acting on these beliefs. Many are variations on the themes of the 'dire need for love and approval' and/or the philosophy of 'low frustration tolerance':

> 'I must have sincere love and approval of all people (especially my spouse, my friends, my parents, my colleagues, my neighbours) about my parenting, or else it's awful, terrible and I am worthless and I can't stand it'
>
> 'I am too old, too incapacitated, too disorganized, too weak-willed to learn new skills or to keep them up'
> 'It's too difficult . . .'
> 'I haven't the time to . . .'
> 'It's a waste of time to . . .'
> 'I'm too tired, depressed, anxious, confused . . .'
> 'It's too boring, too repetitive, too uninteresting . . .'
> 'The teachers/psychologists/nurses should . . .'

We note the recurrent expression of these beliefs during discussions with parents, professionals and among ourselves. We also note the speed with which it is possible to teach people to identify these irrational beliefs and their emotional effects, and to dispute and counter the inaccuracies quickly with almost immediate and positive changes in emotion as accurate adjustments are made and acted upon.

Conclusion

Given some successes in attaining criterion in relation to precision teaching interactions for short periods, we will attempt to maintain and generalize these by modifying and implementing the procedures described. Some of the procedures relate directly to the teaching procedures themselves. Others relate to the way in which the parents describe the situations they face and evaluate them.

Addendum

Since this paper was originally presented, progress has been made towards attaining our objectives. Work is in progress with the family of a nine-year-old severely mentally handicapped girl who was referred as a result of her destructive and aggressive behaviour as well as a lack of compliance. Work is also continuing with B, who has now started full-time attendance at a unit for partially hearing children.

B's mother is now very competent in her use of Step 1 procedures in a structured educational setting, and recently filmed post-baselines of bathtime showed evidence that these skills are being generalized into the natural environment despite only minimal planning. Progress towards generalization was also made when B's nursery teacher asked to be taught the procedures, and began Step 1 work with him. Unfortunately, this contact was lost when B started full-time schooling.

B is also making progress, but it is slow and rather erratic. He is now sitting on request for thirty-five seconds, and will stand (albeit talking) before being given an instruction for five seconds. He continues to use a variety of escape behaviours during teaching trials, but his mother now works through this using physical prompts when necessary. B is also making skill gains in unstructured situations, but despite his mother's claims that she uses the procedures in the natural environment, a functional relationship has not been demonstrated.

Work is continuing on the identification and challenging of irrational beliefs and the accompanying negative emotions in relation to the parent's ongoing concerns about her parenting and B's future.

Work with the S's has benefited from earlier experiences with the

O's and the D's, and has consequently progressed more quickly and systematically. The procedures have been followed as outlined earlier in the paper and the parents quickly learnt to roleplay Step 1 to criterion and are now working directly with their daughter. Greater consideration has been given to ensuring future generalization and maintenance of the procedures, and C's sister, teachers and community nurses, who look after her whilst she is in short-term care, are now being taught Step 1 via roleplay. Work with C will soon begin in a variety of locations around the house and discussion has taken place with the parents on ways of using their skills in the natural environment. C now sits on request and is now practising remaining seated for longer periods.

It therefore seems that with each new case the procedure becomes more refined and systematized, and we are better able to programme in elements which help to minimize delays and setbacks. As the procedures become more thorough, we will be better able to demonstrate conclusive functional relationships between the training given to the parents and the child's behaviours.

Acknowledgements

1. This study is supported by DHSS Research Grant No 0780.
2. The authors express their special thanks to the staffs of Medecroft Nursery and Brookside Training Centre for their continuing help and encouragement in maintaining this project. We are particularly indebted to the handicapped people and their families for participating in the development of the procedures and materials. Among members of staff, we would acknowledge the support of Mrs Penny Patten for giving up time and attending evening meetings with B's family to undertake training in the roleplay procedures and then in teaching B directly.

Research Frontiers

Portage – Eight Years On

Tim Lister

Tim Lister is an Educational Psychologist with the Hampshire Schools Psychological Service.

Eight years after the start of the first Portage scheme in the United Kingdom an increasing number of home based teaching projects are springing up all over the country to meet the needs of pre-school handicapped children. This paper attempts to review some of the evidence for the effectiveness of Portage since its inception over a decade ago in the United States. Hopefully, this paper will encourage those who intend to set up a home teaching scheme in their authority to redouble their efforts.

The proliferation of Portage schemes throughout the United Kingdom in recent years, and the adaptations to school and hospital settings (Cameron, 1982) are a testament to the effectiveness of the teaching model employed in Portage.

In the USA, from the original scheme in Wisconsin in 1972, there grew sixty schemes alone in 1977. In the UK, since the first scheme in Winchester in 1976, there have grown almost one hundred home teaching schemes and some one hundred and fifty projects, if school and hospital based adaptations are included. Many of the adaptations have been described in the proceedings of last year's conference (Dessent, 1984) and in the previous year's proceedings (Cameron, 1982). The purpose of this paper, however, is to review the published evaluations of home teaching schemes in which the parents are the prime teachers of their children.

'Portage' owes its name to the village in rural Wisconsin which was the setting for one of the first twenty four projects for pre-school handicapped children funded in 1969 under the United States Elementary and Secondary Education Act. The project directors, David and Marsha Shearer, realized that pre-school handicapped children, like any other children, needed to get ready for life by learning everyday practical skills. However, many parents were unsure how to teach these skills effectively, and there were insufficient resources to fund 'centres of excellence' where parents could take their children. The obvious solution was to devise a scheme whereby the parents themselves were taught to be effective teachers of their children. There are several advantages of such a scheme.

Firstly, learning is occurring in the parent's and child's natural environment, and therefore the problem of transferring to the home what has been learned in a unit or clinic does not occur. This is a criticism of centre-based teaching frequently voiced by parents. They complain that the child behaves completely differently in a new setting, or that they do not see what the professionals are doing with their children. Even if they do, they are frequently unsure how to translate the general advice offered by the professionals into specific activities for their children at home.

Secondly, there is direct and constant access to behaviour as it occurs naturally in the home. Parents can work on emerging skills as they occur, instead of being expected to work on a programme of skills which the professional says the child 'ought' to learn, perhaps with no first-hand knowledge of the home circumstances.

Thirdly, the maintenance of desired behaviour will be enhanced if the behaviours and skills have been learned in a natural environment. The likelihood of maintenance of skills learned in a weekly visit to a unit or centre will be small indeed unless the parent is shown precisely how to engage the child in practice activities at home.

Lastly, the training of parents, the first and most important teachers of their children, provides them with the skills necessary to deal with new behaviours as they occur. This should be our ultimate goal if we are to help parents become effective teachers of their children.

With this rationale in mind, the project directors in Wisconsin (Shearer and Shearer, 1972), implemented a home teaching programme directly involving parents in the education of their children by teaching the parents what to teach, what to reinforce, and how to observe and record behaviour. The programme served seventy-five handicapped children from birth to six years of age referred by local physicians, social workers, county health nurses, speech therapists, etc. A 'home teacher' was provided for each child and his family one day per week for one and a half hours for a period of nine and a half months. During the six days the home teacher was not present, the parents served as the child's teachers by implementing a prescribed curriculum negotiated with the home teacher and recording the child's progress on special 'activity charts'.

The home teachers comprised mainly qualified special education teachers although three were 'paraprofessionals' with no formal teaching qualifications. All underwent special pre-project training (in the United Kingdom now known as 'the Portage Workshop') on assessment techniques, precision teaching and behaviour modification. All the home teachers met weekly with the project directors for a supervision meeting to discuss progress and problems, and the meeting culminated in prescriptive goals for the children which the home teachers implemented the following week. The home teacher accompanied the parent and child on clinic appointments and suggestions were sought from outside professionals at this time and at more formal 'management team' meetings throughout the year. The management team comprised professionals in the local area with responsibility for pre-school handicapped children.

Evaluation of the scheme was based on a number of measures of the children's progress by the end of the pilot phase. Assessment instruments included the Stanford-Binet Intelligence Scale, the Catell Infant Scale, the Peabody Picture Vocabulary Test, and the Slossen Intelligence Test for Children and Adults. Whilst none of these instruments is useful for clarifying what a child can do and what next to teach, they do represent norm-referenced measures which have been used in the past to represent a child's overall functioning for administrative purposes. It could be argued, however, that the most valid aspect of the evaluation was the progress that the children had made on items from the Portage Checklist (see Bluma *et al.*, 1976).

The results of the evaluation were very encouraging. The directors of the project had predicted that the average gain for the children in terms of mental age on the Catell and Stanford-Binet tests would be six months in an eight-month period. In fact the average child in the project gained thirteen months in an eight-month period. This effect is highly significant statistically. Children who because of age remained in the project after one year were retested three months later. In fact no regression had occurred. This may indicate that the parents continued to work with and reinforce behaviours even though the home teacher was no longer making visits.

Children were, on average, successful on 91 per cent of the prescriptive goals written on to the activity charts by the home teachers. This success can be credited to negotiation between the parents and the home teachers in setting realistic and appropriate goals, and contradicts the strange and unfounded criticism sometimes voiced by professionals who maintain that Portage makes parents have unrealistic goals for their children.

Interestingly, an experimental study comparing randomly selected children from the Portage scheme and children attending local classrooms for economically and socially disadvantaged children indicated significantly greater gains for the Portage children in the areas of mental age, IQ, language, academic development and socialization. It may not always represent an efficient use of scarce resources for Education Authorities to open a 'centre' for certain types of handicapped or disadvantaged children.

Evaluation of Portage services in the UK

In the UK, the first pilot Portage scheme to be evaluated took place in Winchester, and was called the 'Wessex Portage Project'. This is described in some detail in Pugh, (1981). Three home teachers were used in this study, a health visitor, a nursery teacher, and a family service worker. Thus each of three agencies was represented, namely Health, Education and Social Services. Thirteen children took part in the research phase of the project, seven of them Down's Syndrome and a further three with no specific diagnosis. Many of these children were already in touch with a number of agencies, although some of the parents expressed dissatisfaction with the services being provided. The Wessex Portage Project was funded jointly by Health, Education and Social Services.

The evaluation of the project was conducted by the Health Care Evaluation Research Team (HCERT), at that time a part of the Wessex Regional Health Authority and based at Winchester. Their research report Number 125 (1977) reveals that of a total of 236 home visits made by home teachers in the six months of the research phase, there was only *one* occasion when a parent was not at home. On 183 of these visits, specific, task-centred activities had been implemented. The success rate on the activity charts was 82 per cent. The average number of charts completed by each set of parents was three per week, although there was considerable variation, some families managing only one per week, and others up to eight! In all, the thirteen children had gained 37 new behaviours (skills) in the six months, and the research team reported 'the mothers have demonstrated very considerable and valuable teaching skills with respect to the handicapped child with a degree of persistence and consistency we have never experienced before . . .' (Cameron, op cit.).

A further evaluation of the Winchester scheme in 1979 (HCERT annual report Number 154), using different parents and children, showed no deterioration in the performances of teacher, parents and children. In fact the success rate on activity charts in 1979 had reached a figure of 92 per cent, comparable to the success rate in the original Portage scheme in Wisconsin. Cameron (op. cit.) comments that

> assessing progress solely by measuring gains on items from the checklist underestimates the behavioural change that systematic teaching brings about, and similarly to look at the *number* of activity charts set may reflect more on the teacher than on the needs or skills of the child.

The range of variables over which there is little or no control make it impossible to demonstrate that the children's progress was entirely the result of the home-based teaching service. However, all children, regardless of their skill level, made gains in items on a developmental checklist and not one regressed.

Parental questionnaires administered by the research team showed that parents considered that the home teachers had frequently consulted them about the area in which they would like to carry out teaching activities. Additionally they said that teachers always demonstrated activities and ensured parents could carry them out before they left the home. The parents were delighted with the service which they were receiving. The research report Number 125 (1977) says that

> no-one who has seen the changes in these children or their parents' satisfaction in being able to demonstrate these to others would doubt the usefulness of working with families who have a profoundly mentally and physically handicapped child.

Another major home-based teaching scheme in the UK, run along Portage lines, has been in South Glamorgan. The evaluation of the service is described by Revill and Blunden (1979). This was a joint exercise between clinical psychologists working with the Department of Child Health and the Applied Research Unit for Mental Handicap in Wales. After a successful pilot scheme involving eight families, two part-time 'home advisers' (equivalent to the home teachers in the Wessex project) along with their supervisors (both clinical psychologists) received specific training in Portage teaching methods. The home advisers were both qualified nursery nurses. There were fairly stringent criteria for accepting children to the service, namely:

that children

1) should score 78 or less on two subscales of the Griffiths

Mental Development Scales

2) should live within the defined geographical area
3) should not be attending a nursery or playschool for more than five half days per week
4) should not be more than four and a half years of age at commencement of service.

Finally, nineteen families were taken on for the evaluation phase. The evaluation aimed to answer the following questions:

a) Can the pre-school handicapped child be taught desirable new skills using the Portage model?
b) Does the child's rate of acquisition of skills increase while receiving the Portage service?
c) Does the child's acquisition of skills *other* than those taught through Portage increase more rapidly after the introduction of the service?

The children were split into two groups, nine in group A, and ten in group B. Baseline measures of skills acquired on the Portage checklist were taken for both groups. After two months' baseline for group A, the Portage service was introduced. Baseline measures continued for a further two months for group B before the Portage service was introduced. Portage services were offered for a total of six months for group A, and four months for group B, and so recording of progress took place for eight months in all for both groups. There was therefore a direct comparison of progress during the third and fourth months between group A (on Portage) and group B (not on Portage). Additionally, each child was assessed on the Griffiths at two-monthly intervals throughout the study.

The results showed that, during the Portage teaching phase, group A learned 92 per cent of tasks to criterion. Group B achieved criterion on 85 per cent of tasks set. The rate of acquisition of skills increased markedly during the Portage service. For group A the increase was nearly threefold, and there was a similar increase for group B. Interestingly, the main number of Portage checklist skills gained per month which were taught through the Portage service was less than half the number of skills acquired that were *not* taught via the home teacher. This remarkable result suggests that the parents were able to *generalize* what they had learned from their home teachers, which had enabled them to teach many other skills to their children. Individual results obtained from scores on the Griffiths were less conclusive, but the mean increase in points during the experimental phase was four times the increase during the baseline period for group A, and over six times the increase during the baseline period for group B.

The overall results of this study suggest that all three questions posed by the evaluation study can be answered with a very decisive 'yes'. The authors justifiably assert that the Portage system of home training can be operated successfully as a service from which pre-school children of all degrees and types of developmental handicap can benefit. In fact, the pilot project in South Glamorgan has now grown into a full-scale service delivery covering the whole of the county. Clements *et al.* (1980) report that around forty families are visited weekly by a home teacher, all new referrals being thoroughly screened by a clinical medical officer. As with the Wessex Portage Project, there has been no decline in the quality of service offered. The system in Glamorgan has a number of implications for the Education Department as far as consideration for educational placement is concerned. When the time comes for this, the child is discussed at an interdisciplinary panel which meets at the pre-school assessment centre, and this panel includes representatives of the home advisory service. A detailed report from the home advisory service is forwarded with other documents to the Education Department for the information of the educational psychologist. In any event, the receiving school will have details of the child's programme from the home advisory service. The authors conclude:

> What can be stated is that the service works, and that it has been possible without extra resources being made available. The service is also popular with referring agencies as it enables them to offer the practical help parents request, and because the procedures are so well specified, it enables them to know exactly what it is they are referring to.

Parents' views of the Portage service

Mention has already been made of the favourable reactions of parents to the Winchester Portage Project. Holland (1981), reporting on the Lancaster Portage Project, which involved health visitors as home teachers, tells of the following comments made by parents in response to a questionnaire on the project. Parents said that

It provided a personalized service which recognized the needs of individual children.

It helped a child learn a little bit at a time, highlighting his or her skills and giving something definite to do each day.

It allowed them to work at home where things were familiar.

It helped to remove some of the guilt they felt when they didn't know what to do for the best or how to go about it.

It allowed them to work closely together with their children.

The parents who responded to the questionnaire all said that they would recommend the service highly to other families with developmentally delayed children.

One parent (anon., 1981) has reported her views in detail. Her child had Down's Syndrome, and she tells of the guilt and anger which she felt during the first weeks after the birth of her baby until she was offered the Portage service. She felt that the Portage scheme was excellent because it offered something positive for parents to get on with to help the child, when all had seemed negative and hopeless. The importance of the regular support offered by the weekly visit is emphasized – '[it] shows that someone out there cares'.

Which children benefit most?

A study by Barna *et al.* (1980) in South Glamorgan compares the progress of children with different types and degrees of handicaps. The study attempted to test two assumptions:

1) that the rates of development vary between different medical diagnoses and functional disablements, and

2) that the rate of progress is dependent on the age of entry to the scheme.

Thirty-five children were included in the study, twelve Down's Syndrome, four cerebral palsy, four 'environmental deprivation' (some delay but no indication of brain damage) and fifteen developmentally delayed but no specific abnormal physical signs. Six of the above children were visually handicapped.

The children were assessed on scales of the Griffiths before and after implementation of the Portage service. The results showed considerable variability within most of the groups, but that there were striking differences between groups. It was clear that the environmental deprivation group made rapid gains whilst receiving the service, whereas the progress of both the cerebral palsied and visually handicapped children was slow. No relationship was found between the children's chronological age at the point of entry to the service and their subsequent rate of development.

It was interesting to note that Down's children made especially good progress in the area of personal-social development, gaining on average just over one month in mental age per month. It may be that this is a fruitful area for work with these children, since many tend to be undemanding if left to their own devices, and may therefore lack the degree of mother/child interaction in early years which the normal child experiences.

Cost estimates for a Portage service

The report by Cameron (op. cit.) on the Wessex Portage Project in 1977 estimates an annual outgoing of around £5,700 for the entire service per year. This figure took into account secondment of an educational psychologist as supervisor for eight hours per week, and three home teachers seconded for twenty hours per week. Comparisons with costs for offering the thirteen or so children provision in units or 'centres of excellence' are not given, and indeed may not be appropriate, but it is easy to see that the expenditure necessary to offer thirteen families a Portage service amounts to a drop in the ocean in comparison to the expenditure necessary to set up a unit to educate thirteen children. Holland and Noaks (1982), in describing the Portage service in Mid-Glamorgan, offered the following proposed comparisons of cost in providing services for one child for one year:

	£
Portage	400
Special Fostering	2000
Hospital	6900
Social Services Establishment	7500
Special Residential School	5500

The authors do, however, acknowledge the difficulty of making direct comparisons between the cost of providing Portage as a service and any other form of provision. Obviously, Portage cannot replace, and is not seen as a replacement for, many existing services offered to pre-school handicapped children. However, there are instances where the Education, Health or Social Services consider the development of new assessment or teaching units for certain types of pre-school children, when it would make sense to consider the educational and financial logic of investing in a home-based teaching/assessment service beforehand. It may be that existing unit or clinic provision is quite adequate when a home based teaching service exists to meet the needs of children whose parents would prefer to keep them at home.

Conclusions

There seems little evidence for the notion that increased support and provision for the under-threes must be implemented by financing expensive new facilities, as recommended by the Court Report (1976).

DES Circular 1/83 states that 'Special educational provision' for a child under two means any kind of educational provision, '*including support and advice to help parents to help their children*' (my emphasis). The circular acknowledges the need for cooperation between Education, Health and Social Services in the development of such provision. Portage services, through the emphasis on liaison and cooperation between professionals via the management team and through a variety of home teachers, can offer an ideal means of fulfilling our obligations to young children with special needs under the 1981 Education Act. There are few other examples of a system which has been so thoroughly evaluated and which has been received so enthusiastically by parents. The next few years promise to provide education authorities with a considerable challenge to meet the needs of children identified as 'special', and will require the best use to be made of scarce resources. The last eight years of Portage services in the UK can light the way towards a better future for pre-school handicapped children and their parents.

National Portage Survey – Preliminary Results

Sue Bendall

*Sue Bendall was formerly a Research Officer with the Health Care Evaluation Research Team.**

Introduction

There has been great interest in Portage since its introduction into the United Kingdom. More than thirty different projects in the UK were represented at the first National Portage Conference (held in Lymington, Hampshire, in August 1981) and examples were given of the Portage Model being extended into settings other than the home, including hospitals, children's homes, paediatric units, opportunity playgroups (Cameron, 1982). Usually these services make use of tested materials and procedures. Reports on services have produced data on child performance (Smith *et al.*, 1977; Revill and Blunden, 1979; Barna *et al.*, 1980; Sandow *et al.*, 1978, 1981). Some studies have reported on staff performance in terms of professionals' visits, their completion of checklists or their programme writing (Smith *et al.*, 1977; Revill and Blunden, 1979; Clements *et al.*, 1980). Evaluations of parental responses to the services (Smith *et al.*, 1977; Cusworth, 1980; Wishart *et al.*, 1980; Daly, 1980) suggest widespread satisfaction with home teaching services and that they have a beneficial effect on the level of the mother's depression (Burden, 1980).

The Wessex Portage Project successfully demonstrated that a home teaching service for families with severely mentally handicapped pre-school children could be jointly planned, provided

*The Health Care Evaluation Research Team is a group of researchers working under the auspices of the DHSS, MRC, Wessex Regional Health Authority and the University of Southampton. Previous work of the team has included an evaluation of the first six months of the Wessex Portage Home Teaching Service for pre-school mentally handicapped children (Smith *et al.*, 1977) and maintained by the three statutory agencies (Education, Health and Social Services). The project in South Glamorgan provides an example of a successfully maintained single agency service. These two, together with the evidence of the successful educational agency provision in Wisconsin, demonstrate that a variety of managerial options are possible. Despite this evidence there is a deficit of detailed information on the range of managerial conditions in use. Some managerial variables that appear to be important to the maintenance of service quality have been mentioned in published studies (Smith *et al.*, 1977; Revill and Blunden, 1980) and some have been noted in unpublished reports of Portage pilot projects (Daly, 1980; Cusworth, 1980) but there has been no systematic description and evaluation of the independent variables relevant to the successful maintenance of a home teaching service. There is therefore a general lack of information about Portage-type home teaching services in operation in the UK. Planners, managers, front line staff and parents already involved in a Portage-type service have little or no systematic information on whether their service structure is one which will ensure successful maintenance. Likewise those people interested in planning a home teaching service have little or no data on what conditions they should provide in order to ensure successful implementation and maintenance of a service.

In 1982, the DHSS commissioned the Health Care Evaluation Research Team to conduct a study of the extent of Portage-type home teaching services in the UK. The main aim of the study is to describe the administrative and managerial aspects of the different types of services and to compare the managerial components of successfully maintained and discontinued services.

This paper describes the processes leading up to collection of the relevant data on managerial and administrative variables of both continuing and discontinued services, and presents some of the information collected. Although the fieldwork for the study is complete the information is presently being analysed. Full details of the results will be available from the Health Care Evaluation Research Team.

For convenience, the information is presented in three parts, Part 1: Service Identification, Part 2: Collection of Information on Services Identified, and Part 3: Detailed Information Gathering on a Selection of Services.

Part 1: service identification

The initial identification of relevant services was via requests for information to:

(i) All Education Authorities, Health Districts and Social Services Departments throughout Great Britain

(ii) A number of voluntary agencies associated with people with special needs

(iii) All individuals on the Kings Fund List or who had attended either of the two National Portage Conferences (1981, 1982)

(iv) All respondents to letters published in a number of relevant journals and professional magazines.

The response to these requests for information is shown in Table 1.

Table 1: Response to requests for information

	RESPONSE RATE		
	Prior to reminder	With 1st reminder	With 2nd reminder
Individual	59%	59%	92%
Education Authority	52%	71%	89%
Health Authority	71%	85%	89%
Social Services	45%	65%	88%
	57%	74%	90%

* Requests for information to individuals were circulated over a period of time. Not all were circulated on a specific date and not all received reminders on specific dates. The response rates noted for those requests sent to individuals include the individuals intially contacted as well as individuals contacted as a result of information from other sources, e.g., the letters in the journals, statutory and voluntary agencies providing names but no information about the service, etc.

Information was requested about any Portage-type teaching services and their operation in relation to a number of criteria:

1. Families visited regularly at home
2. Forms of assessment used to look at the client's initial skills and acquisition of new skills (possibly a Portage checklist)
3. Family receives written instructions for teaching the client
4. Teaching procedure is modelled for the family
5. Parent is observed carrying out the teaching procedure
6. Baseline and post baseline data is recorded
7. Home teachers attend a regular staff meeting.

The number of services identified is shown in Table 2.

Table 2: Numbers of services identified

	Satisfying all seven criteria	*Not satisfying all seven criteria*	*Total*
Present	116	84	200
Discontinued	8	7	15
Future	6	2	8
Total	130	93	223

Of the 93 services identified as not satisfying all seven criteria, two were future services. On analysing the information on the remaining 91 services, it became apparent that some were definitely not operating as Portage-type home teaching services. Some of the information referred to individuals using Portage materials rather than to services and therefore had no staff meetings, and some were not home visiting but operated from a nursery or school base. For these reasons 85 of the 91 services were eliminated from further collection of information. The details of reasons for elimination are given in Table 3.

Part 2: collection of information on services identified

Two questionnaires were designed to collect detailed information on the services. The Portage Service Questionnaire (PSQ) and the Portage Personnel Information Sheet (PPIS) were designed to elicit information on a number of important variables believed to be

Table 3: Reason for elimination

Reason for elimination	*Number*
Not home visiting	24
No written instructions	14
No staff meetings	33
No modelling/observation of parent	3
Insufficient information*	11
Total	85

* Eleven services provided insufficient information regarding the criteria. The information remained insufficient despite requests for further information.

related to the provision and maintenance of high quality services.

Each service was asked to complete a PSQ giving specific information about the service. The PSQ is divided into four parts as follows:

I Service information, e.g., setting up, funding and area of the service
II Client information, e.g., type, numbers and age range of clients
III. Staff meetings, e.g., staff meetings, frequency, agenda etc.
IV Records, e.g., activity charts, minutes of meetings, home teachers' records.

In addition, each service that received a PSQ was asked to arrange for all members of staff to complete a PPIS. The PPIS is divided into two sections:

I Personal information, e.g., employer, funding, terms of contract, etc.
II Home teaching information, e.g., length and frequency of home visits, supervision received, problems dealt with, etc.

The PSQ's were circulated to all continuing and discontinued services satsifying all seven criteria and six of the services not satisfying all the criteria. The total numbers of services receiving the questionnaires are shown in Table 4.

Table 4: PSQ circulation

Services	*Number*
Present Services	122
Discontinued Services	8
Total	130

An overall response rate of 79 per cent was achieved after three reminders. The first and second reminders were postal reminders in the form of humorous flow charts. The third reminder was by telephone. The response rates, in terms of those services returning the PSQ, are shown in Table 5.

Table 5: PSQ response rate

Prior to 1st reminder	*Prior to 2nd reminder*	*Prior to 3rd reminder*	*Total*
9%	*31%*	*48%*	*79%*

All returned PSQ's were allocated to the following categories:

(a) *Selection pool:* that is, all services whose completed PSQ verified the information that all seven criteria were satisfied

(b) *Uncompleted:*that is, all PSQ's returned uncompleted and all those services who responded to the telephone call reminder saying that they would not complete the questionnaires

(c) *Discarded data:*that is, all services who responded to the PSQ but whose information showed that the service did not meet the seven criteria.

One PSQ was returned partially completed and despite attempts to obtain further details the information on the service remained insufficient to ascertain whether or not the criteria were satisfied. The figures regarding the categorization are presented in Table 6.

Table 6: Categorization of PSQs

		Number		*Percentage of total circulated*	
RESPONSE:					
Selection pool	62%	64	103	49	79%
Discarded data	21%	22		17	
Uncompleted	16%	16		12	
Insufficient information	1%	1		1	
NON-RESPONSE		27		21%	
		130		100%	

Those services that did not respond have been followed up (details are available in the final report). The 64 services in the selection pool consisted of five discontinued services and 59 continuing services. The PSQ and PPIS information from all the services in the selection pool is being analysed by computer using the SPSS (Statistical Package for Social Sciences).

Part 3: detailed information gathering on a number of services

The detailed information was gathered by on-site visits to the services. Each visit included an interview with the staff and at least two interviews with families receiving the service. Service visits have been made to five discontinued services (the only ones that responded) and 14 continuing services.

The 14 continuing services were chosen to cover a wide range of different types of services and included those run by different authorities, those funded by voluntary agencies, large and small services, services with full-time employed home teachers and those staffed by volunteers.

All the parents associated with those services visited were sent questionnaires for completion. The questionnaire covered three main areas:

- the home teacher's performance
- the parents' performance
- the parents' views about the service.

The data collected from the study will provide information about the characteristics of clients and staff in the services, the setting up of services and service maintenance. The data can then be used to look at the current extent of Portage-type services throughout the UK and the relative importance of variables in the setting up and maintenance of services.

The study has already identified Portage-type services in England, Scotland, Wales and Northern Ireland. A large proportion of the services was found to be concentrated in the densely populated areas of London, the West Midlands, South Wales and Lancashire, with a notable absence of Portage-type services in the rural, sparsely populated areas of South West England, Wales, Scotland and some areas of Northern England.

This distribution of the services is interesting in that the Portage model was originally developed in Wisconsin to serve rural areas. A comparison of the Portage-type and non-Portage-type services identified reveals that the distribution of services in the two groups is similar except that there are more non-Portage-type services in North East England.

No direct measure of the quality of the services has been undertaken during the study and, although some of the services collect detailed evaluation data, no attempt has been made to investigate and substantiate this. Some aspects of the quality of Portage services being delivered are included in the seven criteria. In order to be classified as a Portage-type service in the study, a service had to be following the essential components for at least some clients, e.g., written instructions had to be used for some, although not necessarily the majority, of the clients. Analysis of the data will show the extent to which services are following these essential components.

It will be difficult to produce conclusive evidence about the relative importance of variables to the maintenance of services, owing to the small number of discontinued services identified. Information from the service visits will, however, be used along with the data from the questionnaires to investigate the role of certain variables in the setting up and maintenance of services. Such factors as the existence of special funding, the role of the management team and the staffing structure will be analysed. It is hoped, on the basis of this data, to provide current Portage administrators and those wishing to implement such a service with practically-based guidelines on managerial conditions relevant to the setting up and maintenance of Portage services. Full details of the results will be available from the Health Care Evaluation Research Team on completion of the research.

Acknowledgements

All the planning and scheduling for the study was carried out by my colleagues Dr Albert Kushlick and Mr John Smith, who have been involved in supportive and consultative roles throughout the research.

Observations of Mothers Interacting with their Developmentally Delayed One-Year-Olds

Susan Vicary

Susan Vicary is a Psychological Researcher.

Introduction

Over the last decade, there has been increasing interest from developmental psychologists in the study of everyday social exchanges between mothers and children. This has gradually provided greater insight into how babies gain knowledge of the world they live in, and in particular learn about the social world and their place within the scheme of things. The findings generally demonstrate that from the earliest days the normally developing child, far from being a passive receiver of stimulation from other people, actively contributes an enormous amount to such exchanges (Bell 1974). Further, it is believed that mothers and others are tremendously skilful in taking up their infants' lead, readily investing much of their behaviour and vocalizations with meaning and consequently tailoring their own behaviour to integrate with the child, thus establishing rapport and mutual understanding (Lewis and Freedle, 1973). Several observers of early development (e.g. Newson 1976, Turner, 1980) have suggested that this readiness of adults to assume meaning in the vocalizations and behaviour of even the youngest infant is an important precursor to the development of effective communication skills as the child matures. Unfortunately, where the early development of the child is disrupted in some way, certain aspects of the interaction between mother and child might understandably alter. If a baby cannot, or does not provide active encouragement to the adult caregiver, it becomes difficult for that person to maintain social interaction. In such a situation, one strategy which might be adopted by the adult is for that person to take more of a lead in order to keep communication going. Research into the way that mothers and fathers of developmentally delayed children behave in interaction with their children does suggest that something like this is occurring. Jones (1977) suggested that mothers of Downs' Syndrome children are more 'supportive' in their interaction with their children, more frequently responding as if something was meant by unintelligible sounds, and more frequently initiating interaction when there was a pause in the exchanges between mother and child. In another study by Cunningham *et al.*, (1981), mothers were observed to give more commands in task oriented situations and to exert more control over the play of their mentally retarded children. There is a general suggestion that parents are being more 'directive' in their interactions with children with developmental delays than are parents of normally developing children matched for developmental competence. Some writers (Davis and Oliver, 1980; Terdal *et al.*, 1976) have gone so far as to suggest that greater directiveness might be associated with later language difficulties.

Whilst originally my research was addressed to more general questions of parent-child interaction, the fact that a number of families were receiving Portage and some were not allowed me to use the data to investigate whether mothers having Portage visits tended to generalize the use of directive speech to unstructured play situations.

Subjects

The subjects of this investigation were 12 mothers and their developmentally delayed one-year-olds. All the children had been identified as delayed in development before their first birthday, and several, the Downs' Syndrome children in particular, had been identified as children with special needs from birth. Of the group, nine were Downs' children, whilst three had non-specific developmental disorders involving central nervous system damage with some associated physical problems. Six of the group were not involved in any schemes involving home teaching, whereas the remaining six were frequently visited at home as part of a Portage scheme. Therefore the groups were not precisely matched for handicap. It was also not possible to assess the variability in structure of advice given by professionals at paediatric centres, for example, to non-Portage families or the range of rigour involved in the implementation of Portage for those receiving it.

The observations

Observations were made in the home, using portable video taping equipment. Mothers were asked to play freely with their children as naturally as possible under the circumstances, as they would at any time they might find to share during the day. As the study was not directly concerned with mothers' teaching style, care was taken to ensure that mothers did not assume that the focus of the study was their ability to 'teach' their child. In all, each mother-child dyad was filmed on five separate occasions over a one-year period, with an average of 15 minutes being recorded at each visit.

Analysis

The video-recording of data enabled analysis of several mother-child behaviours. However, for this paper data are presented concerning just two behaviours: directive and non-directive vocalization. These two categories have been derived from a number of previous studies which have looked at similar questions concerning parent's interactions with their mentally retarded children, but have undergone further redefinition to ensure that two observers might reliably agree about the categorization.

For the purposes of this study the categories were defined as follows:

Directive vocalization

Utterances of the mother, to the child, which serve to direct the child's attention and include reference to what the child should be doing. Also included are references to locations to which the child should attend and suggestions in the form of questions.

Non-directive vocalization

Mothers' child-oriented utterances which are not included in the above (e.g., praise, affectionate comment, agreement with the child).

It is worth noting at this point that a typical teaching task as described on a Portage activity chart would contain elements from both categories.

Results are mainly presented in terms of the percentage of the total time mothers spent interacting with the child that was invested in each of the defined categories. It was also felt useful to break down this data further in relation to vocalization when the mother was 'near' (within an arm's length plus twelve inches) to the child, as in most teaching activities, and when they were some distance apart ('far').

Finally the data were analysed to establish whether the preferred speech category varied over time, and whether mothers played more nearby, or far from the child as time changed.

Results

A) Time mothers spent vocalizing to their children

There was enormous variability in the amount mothers vocalized to their children during the free play sessions, from one visit to the next, and between mothers. For example, one mother spent less than 1 per cent of her time vocalizing, whereas another vocalized for 40 per cent of the play session. Across all sessions, the mean time each mother spent vocalizing varied between 2 per cent and 32 per cent. Whether mothers played close to their children or at a distance also varied enormously. One mother, for example, spent the whole of four out of five sessions playing near her child, whereas another spent an equivalent time at a distance from her child.

The mothers involved in Portage schemes vocalized more of the time than mothers not involved in Portage schemes when they were close and at a distance from their children (near and far conditions), see Table 1.

Table 1: Percentage of total time observed which mothers spent in vocalizing

	Portage mothers	*Non-Portage mothers*
Near	19.75%	17.49%
Far	8.39%	6.27%

B) The balance between directive and non-directive speech in mothers' vocalization

It would apear that the group of mothers receiving Portage tended to devote a greater percentage of the time they spent speaking to using directives utterances (see Table 2).

Table 2: Distribution of mothers' directive and non-directive speech

	Directive speech		*Non-directive speech*	
	Portage	Non-Portage	Portage	Non-Portage
Near	62%	52%	38%	48%
Far	69%	57%	31%	43%

However, Table 3 shows only small differences in the actual amounts of non-directive speech in both 'near' and 'far' proximity conditions. The major differences between the Portage mothers and those not receiving Portage seems to be in the amount of directive speech.

C) Trends over time in directive/non-directive style of interaction

Further analysis sought to establish whether those mothers involved in a Portage scheme were maintaining their more directive style of interaction over time; this was achieved by comparing data collected during the first two sessions with that collected in the last two. One might expect that higher levels of directive speech were related to experience in the teaching situations encouraged by Portage involvement; in fact the figures on Table 4 suggest the contrary: that the passing of time diminished the differences in directive speech production between the groups, even to the extent that in the far condition the sample of Portage mothers was actually less directive.

D) Trends over time in proximity of parent and child

The final comparison made was of the percentage of time mothers spent in near and far play respectively over time. Again, comparing data from the first two sessions with that of the two final sessions, mothers in both groups were spending more time in the far condition in the later sessions, with a corresponding reduction of time spent in close proximity. Table 5 shows the relevant means.

It can be seen from Table 5 that as the children aged mothers spent less of their time in very close proximity to them. However this decline was most marked in the Portage mothers who showed a doubling of time spent far from the child.

Table 3: Percentage of total time given to directive and non-directive speech by individual mothers

	Portage mothers				**Non-Portage mothers**			
		Directive	*Non-directive*	*Diffs*		*Directive*	*Non-directive*	*Diffs*	
Mother					*Mother*				
	1	6.8	3.44	2.36	7	15.7	7.6	8.1	
	2	10.11	4.28	5.83	8	12.0	6.8	5.2	
Near	3	24.6	7.0	17.6	9	5.4	6.4	−1.0	*Near*
	4	7.4	5.1	2.3	10	2.6	2.2	0.4	
	5	9.06	4.6	4.06	11	6.4	11.0	−4.6	
	6	15.4	7.4	8.0	12	12.6	16.2	−3.6	
Means for group		12.23	7.52			9.12	8.37		
	1	2.66	0.34	1.32	7	6.0	0.7	5.3	
	2	1.18	0.56	0.62	8	3.32	3.64	−0.32	
Far	3	12.6	6.0	6.6	9	2.0	0.6	1.4	*Far*
	4	4.6	1.78	2.82	10	1.8	1.6	0.2	
	5	3.0	4.0	−1.0	11	0	0	0	
	6	10.8	2.86	7.94	12	8.2	9.8	−1.6	
Means for group		5.8	2.59			3.55	2.72		

Table 4: Percentage of time given to directive speech in early and later sessions

	Portage mothers		*Non-Portage mothers*	
	Early sessions	*Later sessions*	*Early sessions*	*Later sessions*
Near	12.6%	12.0%	9.33%	10.92%
Far	6.93%	4.7%	3.24%	6.25%

Table 5: Time spent near to and far from the child in early and later sessions

	Portage mothers		*Non-Portage mothers*	
	Early sessions	*Later sessions*	*Early sessions*	*Later sessions*
Near	78.5%	56.5%	81%	73.5%
Far	21.5%	43.5%	19%	26.5%

Discussion

The primary concern at the outset of this analysis was that providing Portage to a family, as well as producing obvious benefits, might unintentionally have some negative developmental effects. This might have come about through making mothers more directive in their speech when interacting with their children in unstructured situations. The results indicate that for the two small groups investigated, mothers receiving Portage tended initially to use more directive speech. The difference between the sets of parents diminished over the course of the year in which data was collected.

Given these results it needs to be further demonstrated that it is the relative proportions of non-directive and directive speech rather than the actual amount of the former that is important. Further research might also attempt to establish clearer links between parent verbal behaviour in unstructured situations and the child's development of particular skills.

Acknowledgements

This research was carried out while the author was in receipt of an SSRC Research Studentship held at the Department of Psychology, North East London Polytechnic. Financial support for the project is gratefully acknowledged. (Grant No. 580/20880/PSY). Special thanks go to Dr David G. White and Dr E. Anne Woollett, for their support and encouragement, and to the parents who have participated in this project.

The Effect of Portage on the Development of Down's Syndrome Children and their Families – an Interim Report

Sue Buckley

Sue Buckley is a Senior Lecturer in the Department of Psychology at Portsmouth Polytechnic.

Introduction

In 1980 the Portsmouth Down's Syndrome Project was established in order to study the extent of reading skills and their significance for language development in pre-school children with Down's Syndrome.

Fourteen children aged between two and four years at the outset were enrolled in the project. In order to study the development of these children and to study the effect of teaching them to read, a home teaching programme based on the Portage materials was offered to each family.

Seven of the children lived in the Portsmouth area and the remaining seven around Worthing. The Portsmouth children received weekly visits from the home teacher while the Worthing group were visited fortnightly because of the travel involved. Each group contained all the children with Down's Syndrome in the appropriate age group (pre-school) in the area, except for one child in the care of the local Authority.

The children have been assessed annually on the Griffiths Mental Development Scales; their progress on the Portage checklist has been recorded continuously. The children's language development and reading attainments were also recorded on a continuous basis but are not recorded here. All the children were visited by the same home teacher: Elizabeth Wood.

Follow-up on children receiving Portage has tended to be short-term (e.g., Revill and Blunden, 1979) with data based on less than a year. Haydn and Haring (1977) report that Down's Syndrome children tend to make the greatest gains from early interventions during the first year of their implementation and Aronson and Fallstrom (1977) report that the gains made during such interventions may 'wash out' only one year after they have been discontinued.

Previous studies (e.g., Ludlow and Allen, 1979) have suggested that Down's Syndrome children in this age range living at home, without teaching, are likely to show drops in developmental quotients of at least eight points. While these findings may not relate specifically to Portage involvement, they suggest that there is a need for follow-up studies of Portage children to ascertain more precisely what the long-term benefits are.

In relation to these points, it became apparent that although working with small numbers we were likely to generate data that might illuminate these issues further, and on this basis we formulated the following questions for consideration.

1. Was the development of the sample of Down's Syndrome children accelerated by Portage teaching?
2. Did the children visited weekly show greater gains than those visited fortnightly?
3. What factors appear to affect the progress of children on Portage?
4. To what extent was progress on the Portage checklist related to gains in development quotients?

Gains in Griffiths Developmental Quotients (GDQ)

The data presented in Table 1 shows the range in GDQs for the children over the two-year period. Group 1 received weekly visits and group 2 fortnightly visits.

Child 1 moved from the Portsmouth area in 1981 and although she was followed up she did not receive regular visits and the figures for her are not included in the group means.

In group 2, three children left the study in 1981, one of whom (number 8) was profoundly deaf. Although the mother kept in touch with the home teacher, family circumstances did not allow for regular work on Portage. A further two children (numbers 9 and 10) left the study at the request of a head teacher when they started part-time school attendance. As for child 1 in group 1, information on these children is not included in the group means.

While the means for the two groups are not statistically significantly different, it is worth noting that those children receiving weekly visits appear to have shown some increase in their GDQs as opposed to a drop shown for those children in group 2. The eight-point drop in developmental quotient noted by Ludlow and Allen (op. cit.) was not apparent in either group.

As can be seen from Table 1, there is a large range in terms of the change in GDQ over the two years. In Table 2 the children are ranked in order of the change in GDQ together with information on their age and GDQ at the outset of the project and the number of siblings at the beginning and end. As can be seen, there seems to be little relationship between gains in GDQ or age at the outset. The three children who made the most gain all had only one sibling and, for the first two of these, they were of school age. In contrast, the three who showed the greatest losses were from families where babies were born during the course of the project.

Progress on the Portage Checklist

Table 3 presents the progress of the children on the checklist in terms of the number of items attained. This may not be an entirely satisfactory way of measuring progress, as clearly not all items refer to equal size gains but rather to a wide variety of skills and cognitive steps. However, it is a measure reported in other studies (e.g., Revill & Blunden, 1979). It would appear that the group visited weekly have progressed faster on Portage than the fortnightly group; in fact there is virtually no overlap in the number of items attained. Similarly to the changes in GDQ, the number of items attained at the outset does not seem a significant indicator of later progress. There is a significant positive correlation between the number of checklist items achieved and changes in GDQ. Because of the close co-relationship between changes in GDQ and gains on the checklist, it is also apparent that there tends to be a trend for those children with fewer and older siblings to attain more checklist items. A further index of familial factors that may affect progress is considered in Table 4, which shows the number of items achieved in three-monthly periods in relation to various family stresses. This appears to indicate, perhaps not unexpectedly, that such times seem associated with declines in progress.

Finally, it is interesting to note that all except for two children showed greater increases on untaught rather than taught items. It may be of interest to consider further the factors involved in Portage visiting that appear to facilitate learning of behaviour that is not directly taught through the setting of activity charts.

The views of parents on their involvement with Portage

At the end of the first two-year period, all eleven mothers involved at the end of the two years were interviewed by an independent interviewer. While full results will be reported elsewhere, a summary of some of the issues is relevant to this paper.

When asked which aspect of the home teaching had been most important, the teaching programme, a friendly regular visitor, advice and information about other services or some one to talk problems over with, all eleven put the teaching at the top of the list. Nine of the eleven felt quite sure their child had benefited and progressed faster. When asked about the teaching role, eight felt competent as teachers, two did not and one saw herself as '. . . .a mum, not a teacher'.

Seven mothers thought their children learned better at home than they would in some other pre-school provision but five thought that a professional teacher would be better than themselves at teaching their child. Five felt that they could not always find enough time for the teaching and when all were asked if finding time worried them, four reported they often felt worried, six occasionally and one never.

Although the word did not appear in any form in the inteview, five parents said they felt guilty if they could not find time for the teaching, despite the fact that all mentioned that the home teacher never pressured them. The main responsibility for teaching fell on the mother. Four husbands helped sometimes, three often and four never, yet ten of the eleven were definitely in favour of the teaching.

When mothers were asked about the effect on other children, three felt that brothers and sisters had had less attention as a result of the teaching programme but eight felt that their other children had actually benefited.

When asked to choose the pre-school services they would have liked from a range of possible services, all eleven chose home teaching, speech therapy, physiotherapy and pre-school nursery attendance (ten integrated, one special). Only four parents said that they wanted a counsellor to befriend them and discuss other problems.

The high satisfaction with the teaching expressed by the mothers in this group may well be related to the high regard they expressed for the particular home teacher employed in this study. They were most complimentary about both her skill as a teacher and the friendly relationship they formed with her as a person.

Conclusions

It is now possible to return to the points raised earlier and consider what light our data throw on these issues. Firstly, it would appear that our samples of Down's Syndrome children receiving weekly visits showed a slight gain in GDQ, while those on fortnightly visits showed a slight drop. While it would appear that these children have not shown dramatic gains in relation to the normal distribution of all children of their age, it would appear that they have not shown the substantial drops in GDQ reported in studies elsewhere and this result is in line with another study of Down's Syndrome children receiving Portage in South Wales (Barna *et al.*, 1980) which did show some acceleration in development.

Secondly, with regard to the benefits of weekly and fortnightly visiting, although both groups were diminished in size there appears a suggestion that weekly visits were more beneficial both in terms of changes in GDQ and Portage checklist items attained. This is in contrast with Sandow *et al.*, (1981) who reported greater progress over two years for the less frequently visited group in their study. Subjective reports from the home teacher suggest that a good relationship was formed with families in the weekly group and that closer supervision of teaching was possible. Certainly parents preferred weekly visits.

Thirdly, the data from this study suggest that family size may well affect progress, particularly in respect of the ages of the siblings. It seems likely that having other pre-school children and the arrival of a new baby reduces the benefits of Portage. In some homes mothers reported that they could only give attention to the Down's Syndrome child while other siblings were taking a nap. Further discussion of these issues is available in Buckley (1984).

Fourthly, there appears to be a clear relationship between progress on the Portage checklist and gains in GDQs for this sample, although these children continued to acquire as many, or more,

Portage skills without specific structured teaching as they did with teaching. Perhaps the accelerated development is not entirely the result of the structured teaching but also an indirect benefit of home teaching, such as a more positive view of the child's future and consequent generalized improvements in interaction with the child. It may be that such factors may need to be considered more closely in Portage workshops in the future and social and emotional aspects of the relationship between child and parent/teacher need to be explored further.

Finally, parents reported that the practical help provided to the child was more important than the support the parents received. However it would appear that carrying the main responsiblity for teaching their child was an added burden and created some anxiety and guilt at times. This point may also need to be considered in further depth in training of home visitors.

All parents felt that pre-school nursery placements were important for their children, emphasizing the social benefits of mixing with other children, especially normal ones. It is clear from earlier studies that help in the home in conjunction with the educational placement has been an effective service. The parents in our study all felt that the latter was also important and on these grounds an integrated school and home teaching service based around the structure of Portage is likely to be both very effective and well received by families.

Table 1: The Griffiths General Developmental Quotients (GDQs) for the Down's Syndrome children in the Portsmouth Project, 1980–82

Child	Age at out-set in months	GDQ 1980	GDQ 1981	GDQ 1982	GDQ Change over 2 yrs
Group 1. Weekly teaching visits					
*1	28.0	85.7	88.9	93.9	+8.2
2	48.0	63.3	70.3	66.2	+2.9
3	39.0	53.3	55.4	58.7	+5.4
4	36.0	41.1	41.5	37.8	−3.3
5	36.0	55.3	59.8	53.4	−1.9
6	28.0	72.9	73.3	74.6	+1.7
7(F)	26.0	48.8	48.6	50.9	+2.1
Means	35.5	55.8	58.2	56.9	+1.1
Group 2. Fortnightly teaching visits					
*8	33.0	61.2	–	–	–
*9	34.0	76.7	–	–	–
*10(F)	35.0	63.3	–	–	–
11	32.0	62.8	57.1	57.2	−5.6
12	32.0	65.9	68.1	65.1	−0.8
13	32.0	86.5	83.5	81.9	−4.6
14	29.0	73.8	68.5	72.1	−1.7
Means	31.3	72.3	69.3	69.1	−3.2

* Left the study during its first year.

Means are based on those children remaining in the groups throughout the period – see discussion of data

(F): Children in permanent foster homes

Table 2: The gain in Griffiths Developmental Quotient (GDQ) (1980–1982) in relation to the number and ages of siblings

Group	Child	Age at outset months	GQ at outset	Change in GQ	Total no. of Portage items learned	Total no. of sibs at outset	Total no. of sibs under 5	Baby born during project	Total no. of sibs 1982
1	1	28	85.7	+8.2	174	1	–	–	1
1	3	39	53.3	+5.4	60	1	–	–	1
1	2	48	63.3	+2.9	67	1	1y	–	1
1	7(F)	26	48.8	+2.1	71	3	–	–	3
1	6	28	72.9	+1.7	98	2	1y	–	2
2	12	32	65.9	−0.8	44	3	–	–	3
2	14	29	73.8	−1.7	57	1	1y	–	1
1	5	36	55.3	−1.9	58	–	–	–	–
1	4	36	41.1	−3.3	56	2	–	1	3
2	13	32	86.5	−4.6	54	2	–	1	3
2	11	32	62.8	−5.6	47	1	1	1	2
Children withdrawn from the study in their first year									
2	8	33	61.2	–		3	2(1y)	–	3
2	9	24	76.7	–		1	–	–	1
2	10(F)	35	63.3	–		2	–	*1	3

* Newly fostered Down's Syndrome child joined family

y indicates sibling *younger* than Down's Syndrome child

Correlation between change in GDQ and Portage totals Spearman's rho = +0.76 significant at 1% level

Table 3: Portage checklist data for the Down's Syndrome children in the Portsmouth Project, 1980–1982

Group 1. Weekly teaching visits								
					PORTAGE CHECKLIST ITEMS			
Child	GDQ Change over 2 yrs.	CA at outset in months	GDQ at outset	No. of items attained at outset	No. of check-list items set	No. of checklist items learned		Total learned
						with teaching	without teaching	
1	+8.2	28.0	85.7	179	37	37	137	174
2	+2.9	48.0	63.3	275	28	24	43	67
3	+5.4	39.0	53.3	197	39	28	32	60
4	−3.3	36.0	41.1	97	44	35	21	56
5	−1.9	36.0	55.3	179	31	23	35	58
6	+1.7	28.0	72.9	187	45	41	57	98
7(F)	+2.1	26.0	48.8	68	42	33	38	71
Means	+1.1	35.5	55.8		38.2	30.7	37.6	68.3
Group 2. Fortnightly teaching visits								
11	−5.6	32.0	62.8	159	17	13	34	47
12	−0.8	32.0	65.9	199	32	27	17	44
13	−4.6	32.0	86.5	190	30	24	30	54
14	−1.7	29.0	73.8	203	25	13	44	57
Means		31.3	72.3		26	19.2	31.3	50.5

GDQ: Griffiths Developmental Quotient

Table 4: Number of Portage checklist items learned per 3-monthly intervals and periods of family stress

Child	Dec 1980	March 1981	June 1981	Sept 1981	Dec 1981	March 1982	June 1982
1	21	20(M)	15	23	27	45	23
2	13	15	11(I)	22	4(S)	1(*)	1
3	16	19	11(I)	8	2(A)	4	0(S)
4	13	17	11	5(I)	5(I)	3(I)	2(B)
5	4	24	5	4(S)	7	14	5(*)
6	3	11	17	4(I)	22	24	17
7	18	12	14(S)	8	9	3(I)	7(I)
11		12	5	22	3(B)	5(I)	0(I)
12		13	13	9	0(I)	4(I)	5
13		14(B)	1(I)	17	13	7(*)	2(*)
14		8	8	7(S)	20	4(A)	10

S: started school
I: illness in family
A: parent away
B: birth of a baby
M: moving house
* miscellaneous including behaviour problems, family rows and school problems

Extending Portage

A 'Portage Style' System for Supporting Children with Learning Difficulties in Normal Schools

Tim Jewell and Steve Booth

Tim Jewell was formerly a Psychologist with the Leeds Psychological Service, and Steve Booth with the Derbyshire Psychological Service.

The implementation of the Special Education Act of 1981 has placed on teachers, psychologists and parents alike the explicit responsibility of monitoring the effectiveness of their advice and teaching. This is particularly important where children are experiencing learning difficulties in large mainstream classes.

In the pre-school area the Portage projects have demonstrably succeeded in tightening up the delivery of programmes to pre-schoolers (Cameron, 1982). However, many parents are concerned when their children go to school because they feel that in a large class their child will not be as clearly monitored. This is also a concern for class teachers and support agencies like the Psychological Service. We knew from experience that these children frequently require special teaching methods, curricula and materials to support them throughout their school career. We, the authors of this paper, believe that an adaptation of the Portage system will allow us to meet these conditions in normal schools. Two developments are described: a management structure for evaluating the efficacy of the programmes, and the design of the activity charts themselves which take account of the school as well as the home context for teaching.

Management structure

A typical design for a Portage project is a pyramid management structure. (Fig. 1).

Figure 1.

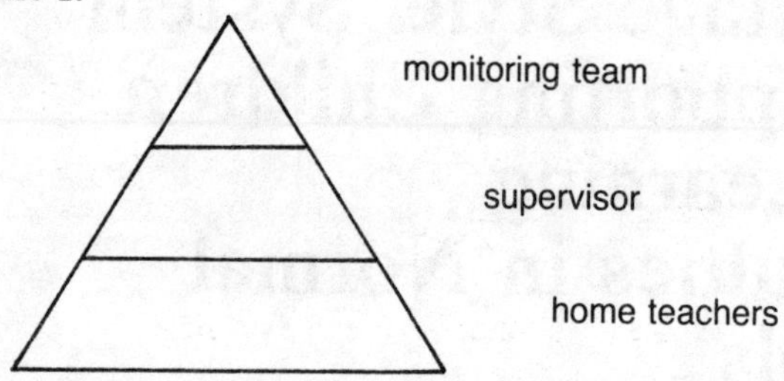

In this system each level of the pyramid is accountable to every other level. The whole structure is in turn accountable to the child's parents for successful programmes. However, on school entry a further level of involvement is added – the class teacher. We would propose that the pyramid be expanded on the child's entry to school. (Fig. 2).

Figure 2.

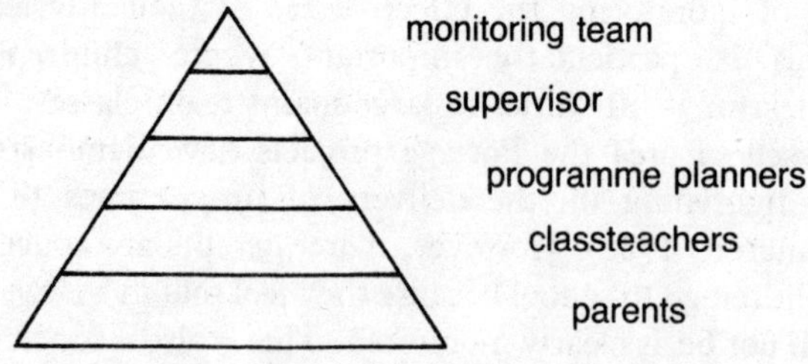

Briefly, the job specification at each level would be:

a) Parents and class teachers would carry out daily teaching of a skill using an agreed activity chart. The child's performance would be recorded on this.

b) The parents, class teacher and programme planners (a psychologist or specialist teacher) would meet once every three weeks to celebrate successes and plan new activity charts.

c) All the programmers would meet once every three weeks, together and with the supervisor, to collate and discuss successful and unsuccessful programmes.

d) Every two months the supervisor would take this data to discuss any problems raised with the monitoring team and to report on success. The monitoring team would optimally consist of an adviser for Special Needs and the principal education psychologist, a teacher representative and a person representing the parents.

Our feeling is that this management system has the following advantages.

i) It evaluates the child's programme regularly.

ii) It provides support where necessary to both parents and classteachers.

iii) It allows for collation of successful teaching methods, task analyses and materials for wider dissemination.

iv) The supervisor would be able to report on these processes to the monitoring team. This team in turn would be responsible for providing finances for resourcing and evaluating the total project with the supervisor.

v) If children were contracted into this system by their parents and class teachers they would not be 'lost'. This tends to happen where children change classes from year to year. Support agencies do not normally visit schools on a regularized basis. The effect of this is that schools can only keep them in contact with support agencies by constant re-referral. The system described here would mean that children would be closely monitored until the class teachers and parents agreed to contract them out of the system or until some pre-determined criteria had been met.

vi) This system would also mean that continuity of curricula, teaching methods and materials could be more readily maintained. One aspect of this is that gains made over one school year are usually 'washed out' in the summer holidays. A support system which had accurate records of each child's programmes could ensure that previously learned skills were practised and maintained.

vii) A body of knowledge would be built up so that people could share successful teaching methods and materials.

viii) Over time the programmers, teachers and parents would collate useful assessment data for the child. This would meet the Special Education Act's demand for assessment to be ongoing.

ix) Successful methods and materials would generalize to other children in the class and, it is hoped, would lead to group techniques of a similar type.

x) Finally, the most important point is that it would allow children with learning difficulties to stay in their normal schools and learn skills for classroom independence. To this end the system needs activity charts carefully designed to incorporate teaching methods that ensure 'fast teaching for slow learners'.

Activity charts

The purpose of the activity charts is to give the parents and teacher a daily recording system for the child's performance. In addition the charts include the following details for teaching:

i) A description of the teaching objective written in unambiguous terms

ii) A list of subsequent teaching objectives that will be taught next

iii) A standard of success that describes the level of performance the child is expected to reach by the end of the three weeks

iv) The reward to be used on successful task completion

v) A teaching script to be followed by both the teacher and the parent.

There are two elements here significntly different from Portage activity charts. These we feel contain aspects that will improve pre-school as well as school programmes.

The first of these is the daily recording system. Two types of charts are used, accuracy and rate. Accuracy and rate charts are used at different points in the presentation of the task. When we first introduce the task and the child is at an initial acquisition stage (Haring *et al.*, 1978) our programme will be one of accuracy. Here the child is given time to complete the task accurately. Most pre-school activity charts focus on this type of programme. These programmes however are often criticized because the child fails to maintain accuracy on the skill and more frequently fails to apply this skill in new situations. This latter point refers to the ability to generalize. Without generalization the programmes we run may be limited in their effect, applying only to the context in which they are taught. For instance, a child taught reading skills at schools may not generalize these skills to the home context. There are several ways of planning against this. One is to teach the skill in a variety of different situations. The second is to encourage the child after initial acquisition to perform the skill more quickly. These programmes are called 'rate' or 'fluency' programmes. After the child has reached 90–100 per cent accuracy on the programme we might then introduce a rate programme to help maintenance and generalization. The faster the rate, the more confident we can feel that the skill will remain useful to the child.

We give a worked example which demonstrates an accuracy and rate programme. Fig. 3 represents an accuracy chart and Table 1 is a teaching script which would accompany it. Fig. 4 represents a rate/fluency chart, and Table 2 is the teaching script which would accompany it. The teaching script follows the same format as those used in direct instruction theory (Carnine and Silbert, 1979). This teaching method has shown positive results in its use with disadvantaged and slow-learning children (Carnine, D., 1979; Gregory, 1983). The teaching scripts include details of the following procedures.

Modelling

The teacher or parent clearly *models* the whole task, demonstrating the skill and giving the answer.

The parent or teacher gives maximum support by doing the task with the child, e.g. saying the answer together: 'Let's read this word together.'

Prompting and correcting procedures

Two procedures are followed if errors are likely to occur or if they do occur.

If errors are likely to occur prompting is used. Physical, gestural or verbal prompts help the child to the correct answer, e.g. guiding the child's hand around the correct letter shape if his or her writing is inaccurate.

Correction procedures occur after an error or no response. In direct instruction, instead of saying 'No, that's wrong', we repeat a sequence of modelling and leading to re-teach the error word.

Testing and reviewing

Finally in our script we must remind the parent or teacher to test the child on all the examples in the programme. For every error we use a correction procedure and later we come back and review these errors to make sure the child has finally mastered the skill. A worked example is given of a programme's teaching script. Much of this script will be useful at the initial acquisition stage when we are using more drill activities. Though superficially uninteresting these scripts appear to be very effective in building up the basic numeracy and literacy skills children will need to function in normal classes.

Summary

The main arguments outlined here are that without activity charts to prescribe teaching objectives, methods and materials we cannot evaluate the education of basic skills to children with learning difficulties. Similarly, without the management structure we would be unable to provide a consistent service to such individuals and meet their special educational needs.

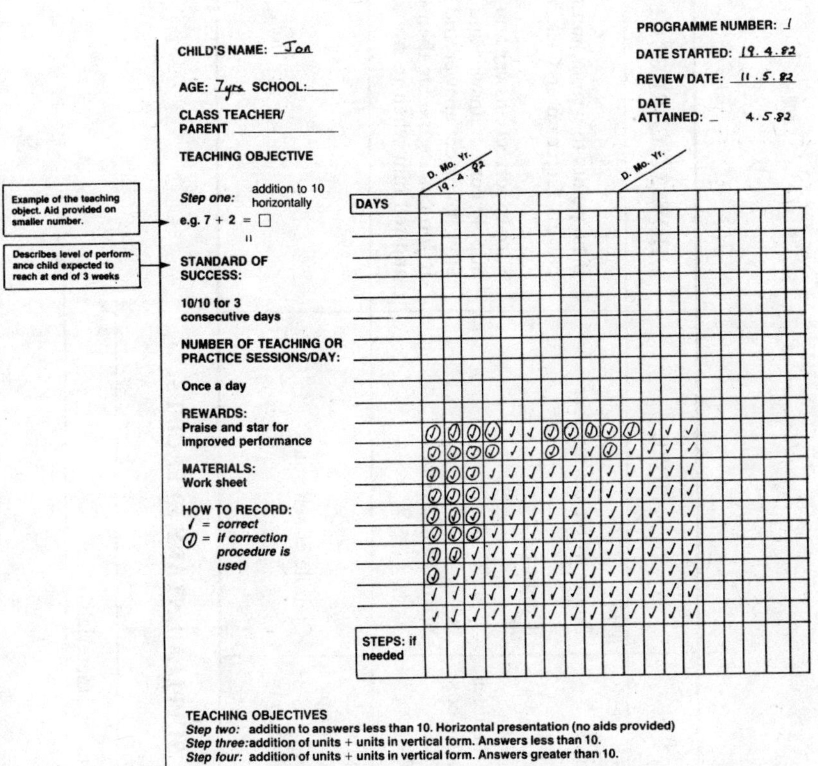

PROGRAMME NUMBER: 1
CHILD'S NAME: Jon
DATE STARTED: 19. 4. 82
AGE: 7yrs SCHOOL:
REVIEW DATE: 11. 5. 82
CLASS TEACHER/ PARENT
DATE ATTAINED: 4. 5. 82
TEACHING OBJECTIVE
D. Mo. Yr.
19. 4. 82
D. Mo. Yr.
Example of the teaching object. Aid provided on smaller number.
Step one: addition to 10 horizontally
e.g. 7 + 2 = □
DAYS
Describes level of performance child expected to reach at end of 3 weeks
STANDARD OF SUCCESS:
10/10 for 3 consecutive days
NUMBER OF TEACHING OR PRACTICE SESSIONS/DAY:
Once a day
REWARDS:
Praise and star for improved performance
MATERIALS:
Work sheet
HOW TO RECORD:
✓ = correct
Ⓥ = if correction procedure is used
STEPS: if needed
TEACHING OBJECTIVES
Step two: addition to answers less than 10. Horizontal presentation (no aids provided)
Step three: addition of units + units in vertical form. Answers less than 10.
Step four: addition of units + units in vertical form. Answers greater than 10.

Figure 3: Accuracy chart

Table 1: Programme instructions

	TEACHER/PARENT	PUPIL	HOW TO CORRECT ERRORS
TEACHING SCRIPT	1. 'Jon, look at this sum.'		
	2. 'Point to the bigger number.'	Points to bigger number	If he points to wrong number then put his finger on and ask him again.
	3. 'What does this sign say?' (+)	'Count on'	
	4. 'Say the bigger number.'	'7'	Supply correct answer and ask again.
	5. 'Count on from 7 using the lines.'	'7, 8, 9'	Supply correct answer and ask again.
	6. 'Which number goes in the box?'	'9'	Supply correct answer and ask again.
	7. 'Put 9 in the box.'	Writes 9 in the box.	If Jon counts too far then you count and tell him when to stop.
	8. 'Read the whole thing.'	'7 + 2 = 9'	
ASSESSMENT	'Here is your work sheet. Now do these like I've shown you and bring it to me when you've finished.' (*The sheet is a random presentation of initial letter sounds.*)	Completes ten sums	

SUPPLEMENTARY EXERCISES

MATERIALS: Workbooks, blocks, money

ACTIVITIES: Counts, adds etc. using concrete materials

Figure 4: Fluency chart

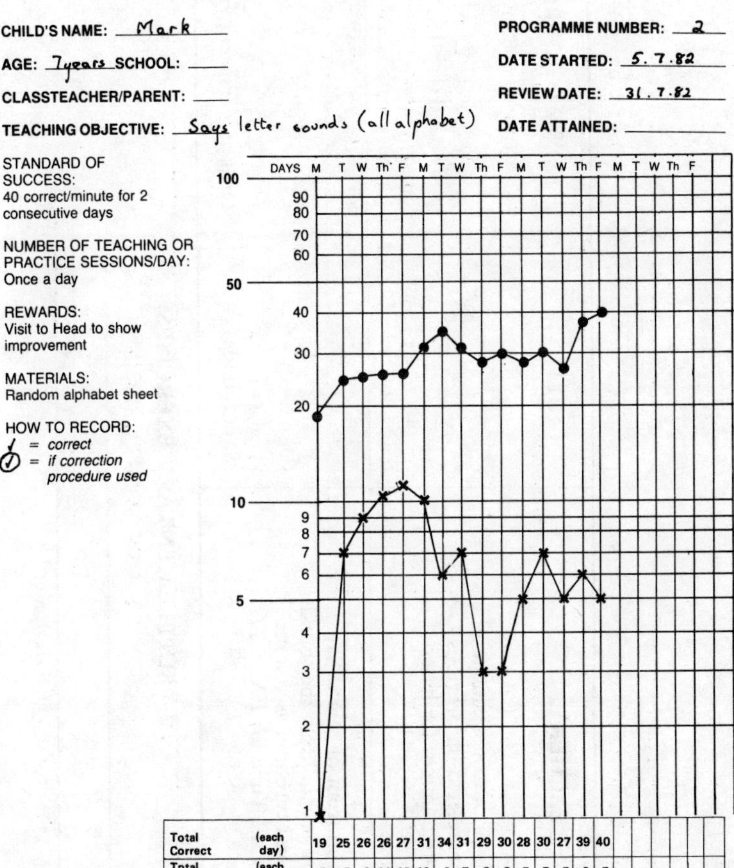

CHILD'S NAME: Mark

AGE: 7years SCHOOL: ____

CLASSTEACHER/PARENT: ____

TEACHING OBJECTIVE: Says letter sounds (all alphabet)

PROGRAMME NUMBER: 2

DATE STARTED: 5. 7. 82

REVIEW DATE: 31. 7. 82

DATE ATTAINED: ____

STANDARD OF SUCCESS:
40 correct/minute for 2 consecutive days

NUMBER OF TEACHING OR PRACTICE SESSIONS/DAY:
Once a day

REWARDS:
Visit to Head to show improvement

MATERIALS:
Random alphabet sheet

HOW TO RECORD:
✓ = *correct*
(✓) = *if correction procedure used*

		M	T	W	Th	F	M	T	W	Th	F	M	T	W	Th	F	M	T	W	Th	F
Total Correct	(each day)	19	25	26	26	27	31	34	31	29	30	28	30	27	39	40					
Total Error	(each day)	1	7	9	11	12	10	6	7	3	3	5	7	5	6	5					

Table 2: Programme instructions

	TEACHER	CHILD	HOW TO CORRECT ERRORS
TEACHING PROCEDURES	No teaching prior to assessment other than that completed on previous Accuracy programmes for letter sounds		
ASSESSMENT:	Place sheet in front of Mark. Say 'When I say "begin", say the sounds as quickly and carefully as you can. Ready? Begin.' Time for *EXACTLY* one minute.	Says sounds	Drill on persistent errors

SUPPLEMENTARY EXERCISES

MATERIALS: ______________________________

ACTIVITIES: ______________________________

Is There More to Portage Than Education?

Susan Le Poidevin and Jo Cameron

Susan Le Poidevin is a lecturer in psychology at the London Hospital Medical College. Jo Cameron is a health visitor, as well as being a parent.

Introduction *Jo Cameron*

I had been discussing the subject of this paper continually for a year through the Management Steering Committee of the National Portage Association. I am now relieved to have Susan Le Poidevin to reinforce what I have been saying.

Last year I published a paper entitled 'A Parent's View' (Cameron, 1984) in which I tried to analyze what I had gained from Portage. At the time, I was training to be a bereavement counsellor with Susan Le Poidevin and as a result I came to the conclusion that my feelings and depths of emotion closely resembled those of a bereaved person. I thus understood what it meant to 'grieve for the loss of a normal child.'

Through this realization, I assessed what Portage had done for me. The trusting relationship with my Portage Home Visitor had been of paramount importance. It was through this relationship that I was able to offload deep emotional feelings and everyday problems on a regular basis, which, until shared, incapacitated my ability to teach my child in a regular, positive way. A full range of subjects was discussed, including amniocentesis, death and education.

I believe that I may be one of ten per cent of parents who have found it difficult always to adhere to the Portage principle of stimulation. Other family commitments have taken priority at times and my own life and my own needs to retain my individuality have taken first place from time to time. However, I have to challenge this figure of ten per cent, not only from my own experience but from talking to other parents. To use an example from Philippa Russell:

her group of Portage families found it difficult to teach in a structured way unless their emotional problems were resolved or eased. There was a temporary withdrawal from Portage but the visits were still important.

Having made the relationship a key factor, a tremendous amount of teaching has taken place and my son Tom has gained a lot of confidence and has developed far beyond our expectations. Portage is an excellent form of education.

It is, however, due to my commitment to Portage and due to my deep appreciation of the effect it has had not only on Tom's level of achievement but also on our rehabilitation that I strongly believe that the supportive role of Portage should not be underestimated or understated. This is what is missing. This needs careful consideration as it has many controversial implications. Susan Le Poidevin will discuss some of these in the paper that follows. Her bereavement counselling course not only opened my eyes to my own process of adjustment, but has given me as a professional, a depth of insight into the emotional needs and problems of people in crisis, and therefore strengthened my confidence and ability to counsel in a gentle, unassuming way.

My fear for Portage and, indeed, for parents, is that unless it is recognized by professionals as having a unique, supporting role as well as being an excellent programme to assist the parent to help the child, this inadequate system of compartmentalizing problems will persist. The situation must be seen as a whole.

A model of disability, rehabilitation, counselling

Susan Le Poidevin

In this paper I will give the backgound to the development of my model of adjustment to loss; I will then consider the wider context of rehabilitation of a disabled person and the family and will present the model of adjustment and a brief outline of the model of disability rehabilitation counselling. Finally, I will suggest a research paradigm by which we could compare a group of Portage teachers who had had an additional element of counselling training with a group of Portage teachers who did not.

Background to the model

Until fifteen years ago, I lived in the United States where I was doing a degree in psychology and training to be an opera singer. At the age of 20, I had an accident and went blind. My family were told at the time that if I lived, I was unlikely to have my sight restored.

I was in hospital for a month. The first social worker I ever met told me I hadn't accepted my blindness because I wasn't depressed enough. The next person who came in to see me contradicted this view, and reassured me that I should not be depressed because 'they' would be coming to break my door down because they could do such wonderful things for blind people now. I went home, and for three months nobody came. The first day I was home I fell flat on my face and broke my nose. After a while, sure enough I started to get depressed. It was something of a self-fulfilling prophecy because when I did as 'they' expected, 'they' turned up. But when they did, the focus was completely on the kind of practical aspects of my rehabilitation that they thought would be useful. How to make baskets and wallets has limited use in getting back to university, and anyone who has ever traded in an Austin Healey for a white cane knows that that is second best.

No-one seemed to understand the changes the blindness had made, both for me and for my family. Especially, no-one dealt with our emotional and psychological adjustment to a suddenly disabled and dependent family member who had been living away independently for several years. Nevertheless, the practical teaching was excellent.

Thirteen months after the accident, I got 40 per cent sight back in one eye when I got a special contact lens. That was equally sudden, and another story. I went to Vienna to study opera, then on to the Sorbonne in Paris. This was a great time of reconstruction. Whilst visiting friends in London, by chance I passed the Royal National Institute for the Blind and went in to talk to them about what they did for blind people in England. They said the rehabilitation training I'd received in America wasn't really available in this country. I thought *I* had felt desperate waiting for several months for help; it would be intolerable if one knew no-one would ever come. Protesting that that was a terrible situation and that something really should be done about it, the next thing I knew was I was being interviewed by an organization that trained rehabilitation workers with the blind. So I spent the next two years travelling around England setting up mobility services for blind people in different local authorities.

I arrived in England shortly after the reorganization of social services, as I went from from one area to another I saw services for the blind deteriorating because specialist knowledge was decreasing rapidly. My contract expired, and I was sent to Oxford University to do my doctorate on reorganizing services for the visually handicapped in England. I was personally looking for the missing link in rehabilitation. Practical aspects of rehabilitation were vitally important, as was the social context in which disabled people live in society. Long-term changes needed to be made so that disabled people could come to be seen as different but equal. But skills for dealing with mental and emotional adjustment were missing in the training of rehabilitation staff and that I sought to find. I worked in isolation and the literature was very limited.

But it was not through any lecture or the literature on blindness that I found the missing link. It was further experience of a different kind which changed the direction of my work and my life. In my first year at Oxford, whilst trying to do creative research, I had three major bereavements within six months when I lost my fiance and both my grandparents who had brought me up. That was obviously traumatic. But eventually it led to a change in the entire way I thought about visual loss by examining the ways in which people adjust to loss and change in general. I was particularly influenced by Colin Murray Parkes, John Bowlby and Peter Marris who had all done outstanding work on bereavement and adjustment to various losses. The theoretical work on a model of counselling for adjustment to visual loss and bereavement took many years for me to formulate. The greatest catalyst for its practical application came when I was invited to become Bereavement Research Psychologist and Tutor in Adjustment to Loss Counselling at St. Christopher's Hospice in London.

I set out to devise a model for other hospices, hospitals and community organizations in how to set up bereavement services using volunteer bereavement counsellors. I developed guidelines for recruitment, selection, training, supervision, support and evaluation of the work of counsellors. I particularly wanted to develop standards and quality control in a field which is burgeoning with frightening rapidity, often without direction or adequate expertise. I worked with Colin Parkes at St. Christopher's, whose work on loss comparing bereavement and loss of limb had profoundly influenced me. He invited me to join him at the Department of Psychiatry at the London Hospital Medical College so that we could do long-term research, teaching and clinical work. From this base, I now give courses on bereavement and disability rehabilitation counselling throughout the country. That is how I got from St Louis, Missouri to the Portage Conference in London. That background is the basis for the model of adjustment to disability that I will present.

Parallels from research for Portage teachers

'Is there more to Portage than education?' we ask. I would like to draw two parallels from my research on services for the blind and my work in terminal care and bereavement which will help to consider Portage within the wider context of the rehabilitation of the family and the habilitation of the child.

First, we need to think of disability rehabilitation as a total process which encompasses all dimensions of an individual's personality and interaction with others, and the family's adjustment to the family member with a disability. Once we are able to see the rehabilitation process as a whole, the second issue arises of service delivery, so that unique and competing needs might best be met efficiently and effectively.

Major arguments arose in the provision of services to the visually impaired about how rehabilitation services should be provided. It was decided by those who are responsible for training rehabilitation staff that practical needs would be met by specialist workers who would be *teachers* only, to teach technical skills and mobility. Social work needs – coming to terms with disability – would be met by social workers. This was a team model of a number of different people working on a 'package'. This is fine *if* all the members of the team are available and competent. But in fact, my research showed that services for the visually handicapped were often incomplete, poorly timed and provided by inadequately trained staff. For pre-school disabled children, services were very often not offered because the child was not registered as blind with the local authority until he or she was ready to go to school. Thus, parents struggled on alone in the early years without knowledge of what could be done to stimulate their children, and without help in coming to terms with the birth and development of a disabled child.

The question arises in visual impairment, 'if all of the members of the team aren't available, would it be better to give additional skills to the people who are actually in contact with the visually impaired person?' Technical and mobility officers, the teachers themselves, often say 'Yes, we should. We are the ones who go in every day to the home, we develop a relationship with the blind person, they trust us and open up to us. It is often in the middle of a lesson that the fact of the blindness hits a person because of the frustration, or a thoughtless comment, and it's then that they want to open up. How can we say that we will go and ring a social worker they've never met to come and see them next week?'

Quite apart from that fact, qualified social workers just don't go in. They are occupied with statutory duties and usually have inadequate training in disability or rehabilitation counselling. I would argue that the same situation exists for the parents of children with disabilities other than blindness. They are often not known to professionals, and professionals who do come into contact with them have not been specially trained to deal with disability.

I believe that there is clearly a case for Portage teachers to have basic counselling skills and understanding of the process of adjustment to disability, to assist them to see the situation as a whole, and to be able to facilitate the expression of thoughts and feelings that impair the parent's ability to teach the child. If you who have a close, consistent relationship of trust and practical help can supplement those abilities, it can only benefit the families with which you work.

There is, however, some concern that if we introduce a counselling element to the Portage package the quality of teaching will be diluted. I want to suggest a parallel from terminal care that would indicate that is not necessarily so.

Counselling dying patients and their families is one element in terminal care in addition to pain and symptom control. Who should be responsible for the counselling within the team? One view is that if nurses are trying to provide good nursing care they have not got time to sit and talk to patients. And yet it is to them that the patient often turns for answers. The hospice movement departs from the traditional nursing model in which communication and counselling are not seen as legitimate nursing roles. In the home care of dying patients, nurses visit the family and patient at home regularly and provide not only excellent nursing care but counselling and support for the family in preparing the dying patient and the family for bereavement. A unique opportunity exists in the relationship between the home care sister and the family because of the continuity of contact before and immediately after the death to help the family make a healthy adjustment to death and bereavement. The example of nurses in terminal care also applies to Portage teachers. If they can provide counselling without diluting the quality of nursing care, Portage teachers can supplement teaching with wider aspects of rehabilitation.

The model of adjustment to disability

There is much more to rehabilitation than teaching practical skills to parents, and emotional and psychological needs can block the ability to learn and teach one's child effectively. I will now discuss the model of adjustment to disability which defines long-term aims of rehabilitation counselling in each dimension of adjustment – the intellectual, psychological, spiritual, physical, emotional, behavioural, social-cultural and practical aspects of rehabilitation.

The process of rehabilitation is a total process. In trying to develop the child's full potential so that (s)he can eventually become an integrated adult in society, the family's adjustment to the child's disability, including grieving for the loss of the normal child, is essential.

In *intellectual adjustment* our goal is to help the family to accept the fact and the implications of the disability: the fact that it has happened, its irrevocability, and the consequences of what that means. It is a gradual process of realization and reconciliation – of changing the things one can and accepting the things that cannot be changed.

In *psychological adjustment* the goal is to work toward the formation of a satisfactory identity and self-concept for the child and the family. Our self-concepts are formed largely by the way other people treat us: The parents' reactions to the disabled child are mainly influenced by their own previous attitudes towards disability and the loss of expectations of what a normal child would be like. The disability is an assault on one's identity as a parent and on the child's developing identity. This is an important focus of counselling. A second area of psychological adjustment concerns the defence and coping mechanisms the family uses which may block the ability to develop the child's potential.

Spiritual adjustment relates to the existential, philosophical and religious aspects of making sense of the loss, and is one of the most important elements of coming to terms with disability. The aim is to examine the purpose and meaning of the event, to find new purpose and meaning in life, and to fit the disability into the way one sees the world and one's place in it. This often involves a crisis of faith. 'Why me?' or 'Why my child?' 'It's not fair' are major hurdles to healthy adjustment. Many workers shy away from the spiritual dimension or denote it as the exclusive province of the clergy, mistaking spiritual adjustment for religious issues only. It is much wider and deeper than that, for our spiritual dimension encompasses all that gives meaning, purpose and values to our lives. Our job is to help people to ask themselves the right questions, not to give pat answers.

In *physical adjustment*, our aim is to maximize the child's physical development and functioning, and at the same time to minimize or prevent stress-related illness in the parents. There is a diverse body of work in adjustment to different stresses and losses that show that within the first year after the loss there is an increase in physical and mental illness, apparently related to the stress of adjusting to the change, and particularly related to the inabilty to release emotional tension. A major, long-term research interest of mine is to look at whether we can minimize the onset or intensity of illness by helping people who are at risk to release emotional tension.

The restoration of emotional balance is the long-term aim of *emotional adjustment* – not by getting back a stiff upper lip as quickly as possible, but by honestly confronting unpleasant reality and the variety of emotions the family members feel without distorting, denying or avoiding them. Confused or distorted emotional blocks are not conducive to healthy adjustment. The need for balanced emotional development seems to be unacknowledged in the Portage concept of child development. Yet parental rejection or over-protection coupled with social segregation lead to emotional insecurity and long-term damage to personality development in the disabled adult the child will become. Some of the greatest difficulties I encountered in my work with blind adults stemmed from early emotional problems, often because parents had not worked through their own emotional reactions to the child's disability.

The aim of *behavioural adjustment* is to help people to reorganize routine and lifestyle. The lifestyle of the family is likely to be considerably disrupted by the handicapped child. Parents must give extra time and change routine to cater for the additional stimulation needed to help the child reach his or her maximum potential. Jo Cameron, in her introduction to this paper, sounded almost apologetic when she said she was amongst ten per cent of parents who could not give their all to the child's stimulation, and in appealing for her own individuality and that her own needs should be understood and met. On the contrary, it is important for her own mental health that her own routine and lifestyle give her satisfactory identity.

A second factor in behavioural adjustment is the need to minimize the number of secondary changes and stresses that the family have to cope with. This is connected with reducing stress-related illness, and with restoring equilibrium.

In *social-cultural adjustment*, we are working towards reorganizing the family and social structure and adaptating to changes of role and status. This is a dimension with the widest implications for long-term social change to bring about a change in the way in which society views disability, which conversely influences the way the parents feel about having a disabled child. There are changes to the family structure with the loss or acquisition of any new family member, but the disability creates an additional risk factor in marital strain, the possible institutionalization or segregation of the child. The lower status of the disabled person in society is difficult for many parents to accept, and much constructive work has been done by parent pressure groups. Again, adaptation to changes of role and status involves changing those things which can be changed, accepting the things that cannot be changed and having the wisdom to know the difference between them. Failure to accept unnecessary restrictions caused by the limited expectations of others is a source of creative frustration for many parents who strive to achieve equal opportunities for their children with disabilities.

In *practical adjustment* our aim is to help the family to adapt to the practical demands of daily living. This is where the Portage blue box comes in. There are many additional practical demands created by disability which can be overcome with aids, adaptations, or learning adapted techniques. Practical help makes living with disability more tolerable, and makes the helper feel better because one can *do* something. But the practical dimension is but one of eight dimensions of total adjustment to disabilty reviewed in Table 1.

TABLE 1: Model of Disability Rehabilitation Counselling: Aims of Healthy Adjustment in Each Dimension

INTELLECTUAL:	Acceptance of the fact and implications of disability; reconciliation
PSYCHOLOGICAL:	Formation of satisfactory identity and self-concept
SPIRITUAL:	Redefinition of philosophy, purpose and meaning of life, making sense of loss, faith
PHYSICAL:	Minimization or prevention of stress-related illness; maximization of child's development and functioning
EMOTIONAL:	Development of child's emotional stability and security; restoration of emotional balance
BEHAVIOURAL:	Reorganization of routine and lifestyle with minimal disruption
SOCIAL/ CULTURAL:	Reorganization of family structure, social structure, adaptation to changes of role and status; attainment of equal opportunity for disabled in society
PRACTICAL:	Adaptation to practical demands of daily living

How, then, can this model of adjustment to loss be incorporated with counselling skills and a teaching package? The model is used as a framework to help you to conceptualize the whole picture of the family. Each dimension is not likely to contain problem areas, but having a checklist, so to speak, of dimensions to consider helps one to see the family's adjustment as a whole, and to balance both strengths – areas in which the family is coping well – with problem areas which require counselling or practical help. Every family is unique and flexibility is required in the approach to each one.

Counselling process and skills

I will now discuss briefly the counselling process and some skills that are relevant to the counselling of families with disabled children.

My own counselling model begins by looking at the overall process of counselling from the first meeting with the parents through to the time when the relationship has ended. I think of a number of phases within that process: Opening, Getting the Story, Summarizing Themes, Setting Goals, Making the Counselling Contract, Working Through Adjustment, Closing, and Evaluating Outcome.

The *Opening* phase is all important in building a relationship of trust and safety which is based on rapport and empathy and allows the parent to confide in the counsellor/teacher. Awareness of the initial impression one makes and the development of the ability to 'tune-in' and be sensitive to the situation one encounters are emphasized in this phase, beginning with basic empathy training and the development of communication skills.

Phase two involves *Getting the Story*, a gradual process of building up a comprehensive picture of the unique adjustment of the family by using specific questions and leading skills to explore each dimension of adjustment to loss mentioned earlier. Sensitivity is required and tact essential in exploring areas which are likely to be painful in adjusting to the birth of a disabled child, and considerable practice is given in asking questions in various ways about painful thoughts and feelings as well as safer topics.

Summarizing Themes is the third phase, in which the counsellor assesses and describes (verbally with the client, and later in a written report for the supervisor) adjustment in each dimension. I prefer to call this phase 'summarizing themes' because it conveys the sense of balance in seeing the whole picture that I think is essential. Assessment or diagnosis, which are similar processes, concentrate almost exclusively on *problems* and can undermine or underestimate the coping abilities and strengths of the parents in dealing constructively with their child's disabilities and the consequent adjustment in the family. This is a process which requires clarity of thought and the framework of the model makes it easier to get an overview of the situation.

Setting Goals is the fourth phase, in which the counsellor translates needs into clearly described, behavioural goals to be achieved to work towards healthy adjustment to the disability. The ability to define clearly the steps that are required to reach a goal of emotional, spiritual or intellectual adjustment is no different in kind from the ability to work towards clearly described practical goals in the Portage package. In fact, this is a skill in which Portage teachers are likely to have a definite advantage over other trainee counsellors who are not used to thinking in terms of step-by-step progress towards a long-term aim.

Making the Counselling Decision and Contract is the next, fifth, phase. It may seem a strange term at first. Having defined what needs to be done to work towards healthy adjustment to the disability for a particular family, the counsellor decides: Do they need counselling? Do they want counselling? From me or from someone else? These are important questions and often difficult to answer. Sometimes those with the greatest objective need have the least desire for counselling, and it is vital to identify those for whom one's skills are inadequate and who require more skilled help. Bear in mind, however, that others with more professional qualifications may have little or no knowledge about or interest in disability, and you may be as well equipped by virtue of the trusting relationship and basic counselling skills to help parents to explore painful thoughts and feelings that block their ability to work constructively with their child.

The counselling contract is a commitment to regular sessions to work on areas previously mutually defined. This phase is already implicit in the work Portage teachers do with parents over a period of time. The model I teach is based on a short-term contract model which attempts to prevent dependency from developing unduly on the counsellor and concentrates the mind by limiting the number of sessions devoted to counselling. This could easily be adapted to fit in with the teaching programme.

Phase six is *Working Through Adjustments* and entails the bulk of the actual counselling itself. A variety of basic supportive and directive counselling skills are taught, as well as other techniques for dealing with particular difficulties in each dimension of adjustment. I have identified Guidelines of Minimum Standards of Performance which the counsellor practises and develops to show proficiency in these areas.

Closing, phase seven, is effectively built into the counselling process from the Opening in phase one because the counsellor bears in mind from the outset that the ultimate goal is to make the parents independent of the counsellor/teacher. Many find it difficult to let go of clients, which may reflect more the counsellor's own need to be needed than continual, unmet need in the parents and disabled child. It can be argued that with disability, unlike bereavement, each phase of the child's life at which major changes are taking place in development requires further input. This may be so, and then another contract can be negotiated for further work.

The final phase is Evaluating Outcome to determine whether counselling made the situation better, in which case those skills might be repeated with similar situations, whether it made no difference, in which case it is arguably a waste of time, or whether, in fact, counselling made matters worse. This we certainly need to know in order to prevent the repetition of the same mistake in the future. Grief counselling can do harm as well as good, which is one of the main motives behind the research I build into all our counselling programmes. On the other hand, there is likely to be a phase for each family during which they appear to get worse before they get better. To encourage the expression of painful thoughts and emotions which have previously been repressed or distorted brings to the surface unpleasant reactions which the counsellor must be capable of containing. Here, the counsellor's own belief in the need for and benefit of grief work is essential.

Throughout each of these phases (which inevitably overlap) the *counsellor's personal qualities and attitudes* are as important as if not more important than any particular school of theory or technique. For this reason, considerable attention is given to developing insight, self-awareness and personal qualities conducive to effective counselling throughout training and practice.

Finally, it is not enough to do some limited training and be turned loose alone on parents in distress. Loss counselling is mentally, emotionally and physically demanding, often draining, and it is vital that counsellors have regular, on-going *supervision and support* from competent supervisors who have depth knowledge of both disability and counselling. In this way, we protect parents from incompetent intervention and protect counsellors from bearing the burden of parents' grief without adequate back-up for themselves.

Comparative research

I am interested to compare the effectiveness of a group of Portage teachers who have been given training using the loss counselling model described in this paper with a group of teachers without such training to see what difference it makes in their performance using the Portage teaching system.

Conclusion

The quality of the relationship between the parent and teacher creates the possibility of developing the child's potential to the full. Combining a well designed teaching model with the counselling process and skills and the model of adjustment described in this paper, the Portage teacher deals with the family in a wider, whole context of rehabilitation rather than seeing the Portage teaching package in isolation. This can only be for the good.

A Problem-centred Approach to Family Problems

Robert J. Cameron

Mr. Cameron is an educational psychologist (Professional Training) with the Hampshire Authority, and supervisor of Winchester's Portage Home Visiting Service.

At present, the Portage model is probably the most noteworthy of all the home delivery services which enable parents of pre-school children with special educational needs to teach their own children in their own homes. The degree of success with which Portage parents and home teachers carry out these teaching activities can be judged by the fact that most of the home teaching is successful (Smith *et al.*, 1977; Revill and Blunden, 1979). These results have been successfully replicated on the hundred or so Portage schemes which now exist in the UK.

Feedback from the consumers has been positive. Parents have said that they prefer a service delivered to their homes (Revill and Blunden, 1979) and they appreciate the help that home teachers provide which enables them to teach their handicapped offspring important life skills and where necessary develop management strategies for disruptive behaviour (Smith *et al.*, 1977). In recommending the Portage service to other families with a handicapped pre-school child, parents have pointed out that home teachers have also helped them to tackle non-educational problems, especially family problems (Holland and Noakes, 1982).

It therefore appears that home teachers who visit homes to offer practical support build up a close relationship with families which not only enhances the teaching which goes on in the home, but also offers parents a considerable degree of 'emotional support'. It is clear too that some parents, for example, Cameron (1984) or Russell (1983), value *both* the teaching component and the help with family problems which a regular home visitor can provide. The need to extend the Portage methodology formally to include non-educational problems which occur within the family as a whole has been increasingly recognized by many existing Portage services. The common observation that some families may need additional support which goes beyond home teaching has been noted by Buckley (1984), and Dessent (1984) points out that home teachers are often forced by circumstances to take on board family problems, a phenomenon which he refers to as 'going beyond the blue box' (the Portage Teaching Cards; see Bluma *et al.*, 1976). Some commentators outside the Portage scheme have almost taken the argument to extremes. McConachie (1983), for example, has made the blanket statement that 'approaches based merely on educational technology will fail to meet a child's or family's needs.' In an effort to place a criticism like this in perspective, the objectives of this paper will be: (a) to re-examine 'family problems'; (b) to look at how Portage home teachers are dealing with the problems at the present, and (c) to outline a simple problem-centred framework which home teachers could use to help parents tackle family problems more systematically.

A new look at some old problems

Certainly, there can be few more stress-provoking situations for a family than the discovery that their child is handicapped. Russell (1983) provides a moving account of the effect of this on a family and sees the advent or discovery of a handicapped child as inducing a wide range of feelings and reactions and putting considerable strain on the family as a working unit, especially the mutual support system which exists between parents.

It is scarcely surprising that families with a handicapped child have been traditionally regarded by professionals as having inevitable and built-in problems. Judson and Burden (1980) summarize the most frequently reported feelings and reactions of parents, which include shock and emotional upset, isolation, over-protectiveness, lack of confidence, uncertainty in handling the situation and so forth.

Certainly, some of the research findings concerning families with a handicapped child would appear at least at first sight to support these professionals' concept of the family 'in trauma'. Although Stephenson and Graham (1978) have questioned their data, Tew *et al.*, (1977) suggested that the divorce rate among parents of one group of handicapped children could be up to ten times greater than the national average. Similarly, Gath (1978) found evidence of clinical depression among a considerable number of families with a Down's Syndrome child and Cunningham (1982) points to the uncertainty which parents of pre-school handicapped children can experience as regards the upbringing of their children.

It is, as Hewett (1970) reminds us, worth questioning this general tendency to view parents of handicapped children as 'guilt-ridden, anxiety laden, over-protective and rejecting beings'. In particular, it is worth re-examining the baseline of comparison implicit in such studies which seems to view the 'normal' family as a stable and entirely harmonious group of people which includes a father, a mother and 2·4 children! Certainly, no-one has to look far to find evidence which contradicts this stereotype. A glance at the most recent national statistics available (Central Policy Review Staff and Central Statistical Office 1980) reveals that more than one marriage in four ends in divorce, more than one family in eight is headed by a single parent and of the 52,000 children in care, more than 37,000 are there because of 'difficulties experienced by parents'. To these figures can be added the evidence from a recent World Health Organization Survey (reported in Moorhead, 1982) which indicated that the number of 'clinically depressed' people in the world at any time varied between 3 and 10 per cent (or 100 million to 333 million people). Perhaps one of the most revealing studies to put the modern family in perspective was carried out by Brown and his colleagues (1975), who rediscovered what many parents of young children had already suspected, namely that 'parents of pre-schoolers are tired, have little social life and an alarming high incidence of psychiatric symptoms.'

Even if we treat such evidence with care, the most cautious conclusion that we could draw from the previous paragraph is that it would be more accurate to regard families with a handicapped child as people who are responding to, and often dealing very effectively with, difficult problems. Supporting professionals should therefore recognize that families vary considerably in the degree with which they are affected by and cope with a handicapped child and that it is important to guard against stereotyping.

A new information source

Most of the information which has been collected on families with a pre-school child with special educational needs has been collected by an interviewer who questions family members (usually mothers). Such data can be difficult to interpret, especially since family needs and problems often change dramatically over time.

The data which I would like to present in this paper were collected over a five-year period. The Wessex Portage Project was first set up as a research project in 1976 (see Smith *et al.*, 1977, for details). In 1978 this successful research project was taken over and financed by the Health, Social Services and Education authorities. The resulting Winchester Portage Home Visiting Service is available to pre-school handicapped children and their families in the Winchester Health Authority (population approximately 200,000). During the last five years, a total of 113 families have passed through the project and a careful record of the successes and problems of each family is detailed in the weekly staff minutes. An examination of this data source reveals a number of interesting features which have been set out in Table 1.

Table 1: Some general details of families receiving a Portage home visiting service (July 1978 – July 1983)

	Number	*Percentage of all families*
Families receiving a Portage Home Visiting Service	113	100
Divorces and separations	5	4.4
Parents admitted to hospital for treatment of 'clinical depression'	2	1.8
Handicapped pre-schoolers received into long term care	2	1.8
Non-handicapped siblings received into care	0	0
Handicapped children who died	8	7.1
Handicapped children suffering from serious illnesses (necessitating hospitalization).	28	24.8

Without wishing to draw too many dramatic conclusions from our raw data, it is, however, worth noting that the number of divorces, instances of 'clinical depression' and children received into care seem remarkably low. On the other hand, the exceptionally high number of deaths and serious illnesses gives some indication of the degrees of physical and mental handicap experienced by the children on the Winchester Portage Scheme.

A new look at the family problems

As can be imagined, the amount of data collected on such a large number of families over a five-year period is huge and only a rough breakdown of the sorts of problems which cropped up over the five-year period can be given at present. Such family problems can be viewed as follows.

(a) *Problems which could not easily be tackled by a home teacher*
The most frequent of these included instances where a child (n = 28) or a parent (n = 9) was seriously ill.

(b) *Family problems arising from supporting professionals*
Although such problems tended to crop up infrequently, when they occurred they also tended to occupy a great deal of home teacher and parent time. Examples included parents being asked to carry out impracticable advice ('Leave him to scream all night if necessary!'), or unacceptable advice 'It's special school or nothing...), or irrelevant advice ('She is lacking in symbolic play...'), or inappropriate advice('Your child is never going to be able to...').

(c) *Problems which were raised by the child rearer*
Such problems were in the majority and included asking for help in dealing with a child's convulsions, managing disruptive behaviour, dealing with the problems of a non-handicapped sibling, providing advice on what to do when a spouse had left home, or in one case, when a spouse had been released from prison.

(d) *Problems which were raised by the breadwinner*
As most of the home teacher contact is with the child rearer, few problems in this category were recorded. However, such problems that did crop up demanded fairly immediate attention since they included requests on what to do when the child rearer had left home, how to face impending unemployment, or (in one instance) the expressed worry that the Portage home teaching demands might be causing additional stress for the child rearer.

(e) *Problems raised by the home teacher*
Surprisingly, there was a small but significant list of family problems raised *by the home teacher.* Most frequently mentioned were instances where the parents were not at

home when the home teacher called (this was reported on fewer than 20 occasions during the five-year period.) Other problems under this heading would include the parents who left their handicapped child for long periods with a 12-year-old baby sitter, the parent who had difficulty in reading activity charts, the parents who said they smacked their child too frequently, the family where the younger sibling might be equally delayed in development, and so forth.

Two general points can be made about reported family problems. Some families on the Portage scheme seldom, if ever, appeared on the 'family problems list', whereas the names of other families cropped up regularly. Secondly, problems which were viewed as serious enough to be raised by home teachers at the staff meetings averaged two to three per family per year only.

Since most of the difficulties reported in the previous section are no longer 'problems', it is clear that Portage home teachers do help families to deal successfully with non-educational problems. Some parents (for example, Russell, 1983) stress the value which parents place on the practical help received from a Portage home teacher, and other parents (for example, Cameron, 1984) have suggested that the practical teaching component of Portage provides the home teacher/parent relationship which allows family problems to be raised for discussion. Certainly, it is interesting to note that other services which have offered 'emotional support' only have often been criticized by parents who have a child with special educational needs (see Hewett, 1970, for example).

There is surprisingly little information about the types of problems faced by families on a day-to-day basis and the most appropriate help needed. *However, it is clear from the Portage data that different families face different problems, that parents can be helped to deal with these problems effectively, and that an ongoing home visiting service like Portage can both pre-empt family problems and also make major interventions such as removing the child from the home less necessary*. There is also some modest evidence which is indicating that home visiting schemes can greatly lessen the pressures on parents who have a handicapped pre-schooler (Burden, 1980; Holland and Noakes, 1982).

Keeping it in the family

It is, of course, recognized that a number of problems raised during home visits are not raised at staff meetings because they are satisfactorily resolved at home, or because the home teacher decides not to raise them for discussion. To obtain some details about problems which were not raised at staff meetings, a questionnaire was administered to the ten home teachers on the Winchester Portage Home Visiting Service. The results of this 'mini survey' are set out in Table 2.

Table 2: Some data on problems which home teachers decided *not* to raise for discussion at staff meetings

Approaches, interventions and outcomes to family problems	*Replies from home teachers*
Types of problems not raised for discussion	intimate personal time would heal
Reasons for not raising problems for discussion	too minor too personal could handle on my own no intervention necessary not enough time available
Interventions carried out by home teacher	gave advice talked privately with Portage Team Member or colleague
Outcomes of interventions carried out by home teacher	situation improved problem got better raised later at a staff meeting.

On average the Portage home teachers said that about 40 per cent of the problems raised by parents were *not* discussed at staff meetings. In the questionnaire, home teachers made a number of additional points. These included the belief that problems should only be raised at staff meetings with parental agreement, that some problems were quite obviously meant for sympathetic listening and not discussion, and finally, that although the feelings of parents about their handicapped children were complex, families could adapt to these.

Helping families: some guidelines

Whether referring to emotional problems affecting a family member, inter-personal problems between family members, or problems which involve conflicts between family members and people outside the family, writers on the subject have no shortage of suggested objectives for supporting professionals. Desirable service delivery features include regular visits to reduce stress and anxiety (Holland and Noakes, 1982); long-term support as opposed to crisis intervention (Phillips and Smith, 1979); repairing or modifying the family's own functioning (Minuchin, 1974), and providing 'ongoing emotional support over a number of years while parents come to terms with their own feelings as individuals who happen to have become parents of a handicapped child' (APMH, 1980). While this list of aims is almost endless, many writers appear to find difficulty in suggesting strategies for attaining these, a situation which has been wryly described by Kushlick (1984), who notes 'There are different opinions on how best these (family problems) should be dealt with when encountered by home teachers, and the strengths of these beliefs often appear inversely proportional to the observable evidence presented for open scrutiny.'

Helping relationships

What supporting professionals mean by a 'helping relationship' can vary from offering a sympathetic ear to helping family members to tackle family problems in a highly systematic way. The different types of 'help' provided for families by the Portage home teachers have included the following.

(a) *Listening to and/or helping to clarify problems*
When parents have expressed worries about problems which offer few or no possibilities for change, home teachers have listened sympathetically and, if appropriate, have helped parents to evalute alternative change options. Such problems have included both immediate difficulties, like the prospect of a serious operation for a family member, or a long-term anxiety about a handicapped child, for example, 'What will happen to Chris at age 18?'

(b) *Providing household or personal aids*
In the Winchester Portage Home Visiting Service, home teachers have, at the request of parents, found themselves negotiating with different groups of people, such as the caring services, the voluntary services and various charitable organizations, to provide back-up equipment like telephones, washing machines, a physiotherapy chair or other aids for parents and their children with special needs.

(c) *Providing information and advice*
Portage home teachers have, on request, provided both information (for example, the rights of parents under the 1981 Education Act) and advice (for example, the most suitable local playgroup for a child with moderate or severe learning difficulties) for the families they visit. While a surprising amount of information can be obtained within the multi-disciplinary Portage team, home teachers have also used the expertise of other supporting professionals from Health and Local Authority agencies to respond to problems which fall under this section.

(d) *Encouraging environmental or organizational change in the home*
Examples under this category would include introducing appropriate play materials into the home, deciding to place heavy, throwable objects beyond a toddler's reach, suggesting appropriate language and play activities for parents and children to share, or negotiating changes in bedtime or feeding routines.

(e) *Teaching parents new skills*
Examples under this heading have included showing parents what to do when their child has a fit or how to control the child's behaviour without excessive smacking, or, most important of all, how to teach their handicapped child important and useful new skills in the major developmental areas. Again, the advice of professional colleagues outside the Portage team, such as psychologists, therapists, doctors, social workers and health visitors has often been sought concerning such problems.

(f) *Systematic problem-solving*
Some problems have such potentially catastrophic outcomes for some or all family members that a systematic approach is

demanded. Such problems might involve the fact that the family unit appears to be breaking up, or an older sibling has committed a minor crime, or a child in the family has a terminal illness, or an adult in the family has been given a medium-term prison sentence. In the remainder of this paper I would like to describe a method which could be used to deal with these more serious problems.

A problem-centred approach

Howarth (1980) has suggested that it might be more useful to regard families as 'problem-solvers' and supporting professionals who provide a service as 'facilitators of solutions to problems'. While this is a good theoretical stance to adopt, the practical task of turning family members into 'problem-solvers' is not without its difficulties.

Indeed, a number of writers have suggested that people are usually not very good at problem-solving. Miller *et al.*, (1960) make the important point that 'an ordinary person almost never approaches problems systematically and exhaustively unless specifically educated to do so.' Similarly, Carnine and Silbert (1979) and Papert (1980) have argued that our culture is relatively poor in systematic models for solving problems and such methods as do exist are rarely taught (people are obviously expected to pick them up either from experience or by osmosis!) There is, however, as D'Zurilla and Goldfried (1971) have shown increasing evidence that problem-solving skills can be taught successfully 'if they are taught directly'.

In origin, the problem-centred approach to be explored in this paper derives from a behavioural case work procedure developed in the U.S. (Thomas and Walter, 1973), which has also been employed by the Wessex Health Care Evaluation Research Team (see Nixon, 1976). In developing this model at Southampton University, we have been guided by the constructional (as opposed to the diagnostic) approach to problems advocated by Schwartz and Goldiamond, (1975). It must also be noted that Cullen *et al.* (1982) and Howarth (1980) describe models which have some features similar to those of the problem-centred approach.

The approach which is described in Table 3 has two objectives. It provides an easy and self-correcting method which home teachers could use and it is also designed to allow users to step back from problem situations and to view them more objectively. The attraction of the problem-centred approach is that there is an easy to follow, carefully sequenced series of steps which enables the user(s) to move from problem to intervention to evaluation of effectiveness. Incidentally, this deceptively simple model has shown itself robust enough to deal with the problems of individuals (Cameron and Stratford, 1978) as well as organizational problems (Stratford and Cameron, 1979). A detailed description of the model for parents and teachers has been provided by Westmacott and Cameron (1981) and its importance in the field of applied psychology training has recently been discussed (see Cameron and Stratford, 1983).

Possible advantages

Although no-one would claim that the model described could be used to solve every family problem, it does offer a number of advantages.

(1) This approach could be quickly taught to both home teachers and parents.

(2) The problem-centred approach focuses on features of a problem situation which *can* be changed. In other words, 'problems' and not 'people' become the focus of change.

(3) The approach does not violate the principle of minimal intervention, or in other words when dealing with a problem it generates simple strategies first before moving on to more complex ones.

(4) This approach recognizes that the problem solutions are most likely to lie within the competence of the person(s) who originally stated the problem.

Table 3: The ten steps which can be followed when helping the client(s) to examine problems more objectively with a view to changing a problem situation: the problem centred approach

STEP 1.	List *assets* and areas of *favourable progress* (i.e., 'things which are going well'.)
STEP 2.	List *problems, complaints* and *difficulties.*
STEP 3.	Establish an order of priorities among the problem areas to be dealt with and choose a *priority problem.* Note that a priority problem may be 'a problem to start working on' or 'the most critical or pressing problem' or even 'the problem most likely to improve quickly'. This decision is made by the client(s).

STEP 4. Arrive at an *operational definition of the priority problem.* This means helping the client(s) to specify clearly, 'what happens when...?' or 'what precisely is meant by...?' or 'what examples do we have...?' In other words fuzzy or unclear descriptions of the priority problem are to be avoided as much as possible.

STEP 5. Collect *information* on either the frequency (how often?) the magnitude (how great?) or the duration (how long?) of the priority problem. Look for clearly observable features of the priority problem rather than impressions, intuitions or insights.

STEP 6. Discuss what *factors* may be contributing to the priority problem. Consider the antecedent (before), background (during) and consequent (after) events which surround the priority problem. It is helpful to (a) avoid labels or pseudo explanations and (b) focus discussion on those controlling conditions which can be changed.

STEP 7a. Discuss and agree a *desired outcome to the* priority problem, i.e. what would be happening if the priority problem was alleviated reduced or satisfactorily overcome.

STEP 7b. Check that attaining the desired outcome would alleviate the priority problem described in Step 4.

STEP 7c. Ensure that the desired outcome specified does not conflict with the objectives of other people (e.g., supporting professionals) or with the family as a whole.

STEP 8a. Plan and agree a course of action (*an intervention*) to reach the objective/desired outcome described in Step 7c. Again, check that this intervention is not incompatible with the objectives of other people (including those within the family).

STEP 8b. *Implement the course of action* after providing (a) clear directions on how to carry out the plan of action (b) if necessary, modelling the intervention for client(s) and (c) agreeing who will record progress, what they will record and what follow up is necessary.

STEP 9. *Record* and *monitor* the course of action and report back on progress.

STEP 10a. If the agreed course of action was *successful*, celebrate its success and either agree with the client(s) that no further help is needed or choose another problem from the original list in Step 2 and repeat steps 3–9.

STEP 10b. If the outcome was *unsuccessful*, then several options are open. These include reconsidering the factors affecting the problem (Step 6), revising and setting a more realistic desired outcome (Step 7), or agreeing a different course of action (Step 8) and again proceeding through the remainder of the ten steps.

Some conclusions

Problems experienced by families in general have traditionally been regarded as highly complex and when a family has included a handicapped child, then supporting professionals have often believed that the complexity of family problems increased exponentially. It is likely that the practical help brought to parents by Portage home teachers has pre-empted many family problems. The problem-centred approach described, while recognizing the uniqueness of both a family and its members, may offer them opportunities both to build on successes offered by the teaching component of the Portage Scheme and at the same time arrive at their own strategies for changing other problem situations in the home.

In essence, the problem-centred approach allows parents and home teachers to consider more objectively the functional relationship between the problem and its controlling events in a way which fits in which the existing home *teaching* service. In other words, the approach being advocated here can be used to supplement (as opposed to supplant) the existing home teaching services based on the Portage model.

Bibliography

ANONYMOUS MOTHER OF A DOWN'S SYNDROME BABY (1981). 'Portage – a parent's view', *Health Visitor*, November, **54**, 488–9.

ARONSON, M. and FALLSTROM, A. (1977). 'Immediate and long-term effects of developmental training in children with Down's Syndrome', *Developmental Medicine and Child Neurology*, **19**, 489–94.

ASSOCIATION OF PROFESSIONS FOR THE MENTALLY HANDICAPPED (APMH) (1980). *Mental Handicap: The Under-Fives*. Report of a Conference at the King's Fund Centre, November 1980. London: APMH.

BARNA, S., BIDDER, R.T., GRAY, O.P., CLEMENTS, J. and GARDENER, J. (1980). 'The progress of developmentally delayed pre-school children in a home training scheme', *Child: Care, Health and Development*, **6**, 157–64.

BECK, A.T. (1976). *Cognitive Therapy and the Emotional Disorders*. New York: International University Press.

BELL, I.P. (1979). 'Towards a language curriculum for the ESN(S) school', *Apex, Journal of the British Institute of Mental Handicap*, **7**, 1, 10–12.

BELL, R.Q. (1974). 'Contribution of human infants to caregiving and social interaction'. In: LEWIS, M. and ROSENBLAM, L.A. (Eds) *The Effects of the Infant on its Caregiver*. New York: Wiley and Sons.

BENDALL, S.A., SMITH, J. and KUSHLICK, A. (1983). *National Study of Portage Type Home Teaching Services. Vols I, II, and III*. Report 162. Health Care Evaluation Research Team: University of Southampton.

BENDER, M., VALLETUTTI, P.J. and BENDER R. (1976). *Teaching the Moderately and Severely Handicapped: Curriculum Objectives, Strategies and Activities. Vols I, II and III*. Baltimore, London, Tokyo: University Park Press.

BIRMINGHAM INNER CITY PARTNERSHIP (1982). Birmingham Inner Profile. Birmingham: Birmingham Inner City Partnership.

BLUMA, S.M., SHEARER, M.S., FROHMAN, A.H. and HILLIARD, J.M. (1976). *Portage Guide to Early Education*. CESA: 12, Portage, Wisconsin. Available through NFER-NELSON: Windsor.

BOYD, R.D. and BLUMA, S.M. (1977). *Portage Parent Programme: Parent Readings*. Windsor: NFER-NELSON.

BRAIN, M.D.S. (1976). Children's First Word Combinations. Monographs of the Society for Research in Child Development, **41**, 1, Serial No. 164.

BRINKWORTH, R. (1975). 'The unfinished child: early treatment and training for the infant with Down's Syndrome', *Royal Society of Health*, **2,** 73.

BRONFENBRENNER, U. (1976). 'Is early intervention effective?' In: CLARKE, A.M., and CLARKE, A.D. (Eds) *Early Experiences: Myth and Evidence*. Shepton Mallet: Open Books Publishing Ltd. (Distributors: Dent.)

BROSNAN, D., and HUGGETT, S.A. (1984). 'From checklists to curriculum: using Portage as a basis for curriculum development in a nursery school'. In: DESSENT, A.R. (Ed). *What is Important about Portage?* Windsor: NFER-NELSON.

BROWN, G.W., NI BHROLCHAIN, M. and HARRIS, T. (1975). 'Social Class and psychiatric disturbance among women in an urban population', *Sociology*, **9,** 225–53.

BUCKLEY, S. (1984). 'The influence of family variables on children's progress on Portage'. In: DESSENT, A. (Ed) *What is Important about Portage?* Windsor: NFER-NELSON.

BULLOCK REPORT. GREAT BRITAIN. DEPARTMENT OF EDUCATION AND SCIENCE (1975). *A Lanuage for Life*. London: HMSO.

BURDEN, R.L. (1978). 'An approach to the evaluation of early intervention projects with mothers of severely handicapped children: the attitude dimension', *Child: Care, Health and Development*, **4,** 171–181.

BURDEN, R.L. (1979). 'Intervention programmes with families of handicapped children', *Bulletin of the British Psychological Society*, **32,** 137–41.

BURDEN, R.L. (1980). 'Measuring the effects of stress on the mothers of handicapped infants: must depression always follow?' *Child: Care, Health and Development*, **6,** 111–25.

CAMERON, J. (1984). 'A parent's view of Portage'. In: DESSENT, A. (Ed) *What is Important about Portage?* Windsor: NFER-NELSON.

CAMERON, R.J. (Ed) (1982). *Working Together: Portage in the UK*. Windsor: NFER-NELSON.

CAMERON, R.J. and STRATFORD, R.J. (1978). 'Target practice: preparing accountable educational psychologists', British Psychological Society (Division of Educational and Child Psychologists) *DECP Occasional Papers*, **2,** 1, 27–32.

CAMERON, R.J. and STRATFORD, R.J. (1983). 'A problem centred approach to the delivery of applied psychology services', accepted by the *Journal of the Association of Eductional Psychologists* (in print).

CARLYLE, J. (1980). 'A paediatric home therapy programme for developmental progress in severely handicapped infants', *Child: Care, Health and Development*, **6,** 6.

CARNINE, D. (1979). 'Direct instruction: a successful system for educationally high risk children', *Journal of Curriculum Studies*, **11,** 1.

CARNINE, D. and SILBERT, J. (1979). *Direct Instruction Reading*. Columbus, Ohio: Charles E. Merrill.

CASTILLO, M., SMITH, J., GLOSSOP, C. and KUSHLICK, A. (1979). *The Wessex Portage Project: Maintenance after Three Years*. Research Report No. 154. University of Southampton: Health Care Evaluation Research Team.

CLEMENTS, J., BIDDER, R., GARDNER, S., BRYANT, G. and GRAY, O.P. (1980). 'A home advisory service for pre-school children with developmental delay', *Child: Care, Health and Development*, **6,** 25–33.

CLEMENTS, S.C., SMITH, I., SPAIN, B. and WATKEYS, I. (1982). 'A preliminary investigation on the use of the Portage system in day nurseries', *Child: Care, Health and Development*, **8,** 123–31.

CLUNIES-ROSS, G.G. (1979). 'Accelerating the development of Down's Syndrome infants and young children', *Journal of Special Education*, **13,** 2, 169–77.

COURT REPORT. GREAT BRITAIN. DEPARTMENT OF EDUCATION AND SCIENCE (1976). *Fit for the Future*. London: HMSO.

CULLEN, C., BURTON, M., and THOMAS, M. (1982). 'A model for behaviour analysis in mental handicap', *Journal of Practical Approaches to Developmental Handicap*, **6,** 1, 6–9.

CUNNINGHAM, C.C. (1975). 'Parents as therapists and educators'. In: KIERNAN, V., WOODFORD, F.P. (Eds) *Behaviour Modification with the Severely Retarded Study Group 8*. Amsterdam: Scientific Publishers.

CUNNINGHAM, C.C. (1980). 'Psychological and educational aspects of handicap'. Paper presented to the International Symposium on Inborn Errors of Metabolism in Humans, Interlaken: Hester Adrian Reserch Centre.

CUNNINGHAM, C.C. (1982). *Down's Syndrome: an Introduction for Parents*. London: Souvenir Press.

CUNNINGHAM, C., RUELER, E., BLACKWELL, J. and BECK, K. (1981). 'Behavioural and linguistic developments in the interactions of normal and Down's retarded children with their mothers', *Child Development*, **52,** 62–70.

CUSWORTH, S.A. (1980). *Kirklees Pre-Pilot Portage Evaluation Report*. Huddersfield: Kirklees Education Department.

CYSTER, R., CLIFT, P.S. and BATTLE, S. (1979). *Parental Involvement in Primary Schools*. Windsor: NFER-NELSON.

DALY, B. (1980). *Evaluation of Portage Home Teaching Pilot Project for Pre-school Handicapped Children*. Report P/S02. Barking and Dagenham Schools Psychological Service.

DAVENPORT, E. (1983). The Play of Sikh Children in a Nursery Class and at Home. Unpublished manuscript.

DAVIS, H. and OLIVER, B. (1980). 'A comparison of aspects of the maternal speech environment of retarded and non-retarded children', *Child: Care, Health and Development*, **6,** 135–45.

DE CORIAT, L., THESLENCO, L., WAKSMAN, J. (1968). 'The effects of psychomotor stimulation of the IQ of young children with Trisomy 21'. In: RICHARDS, B.W. (Ed) *Proceedings of the 1st Conference of the International Association for the Scientific Study of Mental Deficiency*. Reigate: Jackson Publishing Company.

DESSENT, A. (Ed) (1984). *What is Important About Portage?* Windsor: NFER-NELSON.

D'ZURILLA, T.J. and GOLDFRIED, M.R. (1971). 'Problem solving and behaviour modification', *Journal of Abnormal Psychology*, **77,** 107–126.

ELLIS, A. (1962). *Reason and Emotion in Psychotherapy*. New York: Lyle Stuart.

ELLIS, A, and HARPER, R.A. (1975). *A New Guide to Rational Living*. Hollywood: Wilshire Book Co.

FELCE, D., de KOCK, U., MANSELL, J. and JENKINS, J. (in press). 'Providing systematic individual teaching for severely disturbed and profoundly mentally handicapped adults in residential care', *Behaviour Research and Therapy*.

FENN, G. (1976). 'A language teaching programme for severely subnormal children'. In: British Institute of Mental handicap (IMS) conference proceedings *Language and the Mentally Handicapped – 2*. BIMH. (out of print).

GARDENER, J.M. (1980). *Developmentally Sequenced Checklist of the Portage Guide to Early Education*. Walsall: Walsall School Psychological Service.

GATH, A. (1978). *Down's Syndrome and the Family*. London: Academic Press.

GHUMAN, P.A.S. (1975). *The Cultural Context of Thinking*. Windsor: NFER-NELSON.

GILLHAM, B. (1979). *The First Words Language Programme*. London: George Allen and Unwin.

GILLHAM, B. (1981). The development and evaluation of a language remediation programme for mentally handicapped children. Unpublished PhD thesis. University of Nottingham.

GILLHAM, B. (1982). *The First Sentences Book Cards*. Wisbech: Learning Development Aids (LDA).

GILLHAM, B. (1983). *The Words Together: A First Sentences Language Programme*. London: George Allen and Unwin.

GREAT BRITAIN. CENTRAL POLICY REVIEW STAFF AND CENTRAL STATISTICAL OFFICE (1980). *People and their Families*. London: HMSO.

GREAT BRITAIN. DEPARTMENT OF EDUCATION AND SCIENCE. Circular 1/83. *Assessments and Statements of Special Eductional Needs*. Available from the Department of Education and Science, Honeypot Lane, Canons Park, Stanmore, Middlesex.

GREGORY, R.P. (1983). 'Direct instruction, disadvantaged and handicapped children: a review of the literature and some practical implications' (Parts I and II), *Remedial Education*, **18**, 3.

HARING, N., LOVITT, T., EATON, M. and HANSON. (1978). *The Fourth R – Research in the Classroom*. Columbus, Ohio: Charles E. Merrill.

HAYDN, A.H. and DIMITRIEV. (1975). 'Early development and educational problems for the child with Down's Syndrome'. In: FRIEDLANDER, B. (Ed) *The Exceptional Infant, Vol III*. New York: Brunner/Mazel.

HAYDN, A.H. and HARING, N.G. (1977). 'The acceleration and maintenance of developmental gains in Down's Syndrome school-age children'. In: MITTLER, P. (Ed) *Research to Practice in Mental*

Retardation, Vol I. Baltimore: University Park Press.

HENLEY, A. (1979). *Asian Patients in Hospital and at Home*. London: Kings Fund Publications.

HEWETT, S. (1970). *The Family and the Handicapped Child*. London: George Allen and Unwin.

HOLLAND, F.L.V. and NOAKS, J.C. (1982). 'Portage in mid-Glamorgan: description and comment on this pre-school home intervention scheme', *Journal of Association of Educational Psychologists*, 5, 9, 32–7.

HOLLAND, J. (1981). 'The Lancaster Portage Project: a home-based service for developmentally delayed young children and their families', *Health Visitor*, 54.

HOWARTH, C.J. (1980). 'The structure of effective psychology: man as a problem solver'. In: CHAPMAN, A.J. and JONES, D.M. (Eds) *Models of Man*. Leicester: British Psychology Society.

JONES, O.H.M. (1977). 'Mother-child communication with pre-school linguistic Down's Syndrome and normal infants'. In: SCHAFFER, H.R. (Ed) *Studies in Mother-Child Interaction*. London: Academic Press.

JOSE, R.T., SMITH, A.H., and SHANE, G.S. (1980). 'Evaluating and stimulating vision in the multiply impaired', *Journal of Visual Impairment and Blindness*, Jan 1980. 2–8.

JUDSON, S., and BURDEN, R.L. (1980). 'Towards a tailored measure of parental attitudes: an approach to the evaluation of one aspect of intervention projects with parents of handicapped children', *Child: Care, Health and Development*, **6**, 1, 47–57.

KOGEL, R.L., RUSSO, D.C. and RINCOVER, A. (1977). 'Assessing and training teachers in the generalized use of behaviour modification with autistic children', *Journal of Applied Behavior Analysis*, **10**, 197–205.

KOEGEL, R.L., GLAHN, T.J. and NIEMINEN, G.W.(1978). 'Generalization of parent-training results', *Journal of Applied Behavior Analysis*, **11**, 95–109.

KOEGEL, R.L., EGEL, A.L. and WILLIAMS, J.A. (1980). 'Behavioural contrast and generalization across settings in the treatment of autistic children', *Journal of Experimental Child Psychiatry*, **30**, 422–47.

KUSHLICK, A. (1984). 'A national Portage Association (UK)?' In: DESSENT, A. (Ed) *What is Important about Portage?* Windsor: NFER-NELSON.

KUSHLICK, A. and SMITH, J. (1982). Domiciliary Interventions in Families with Severely Mentally Handicapped Children and Young Adults. Application for a Research Grant to the DHSS, London.

LENNENBERG, E.H. (1967). *Biological Foundations of Language*. New York: Wiley.

LEVENSTEIN, P. and SUNLEY, R. (1968). 'Stimulation of verbal interaction between disadvantaged mothers and children', *American Journal of Orthopsychiatry*, **38**, 116–121.

LEWIS, M. and FREEDLE, R. (1973). 'Mother-infant dyad: the cradle of meaning'. In PLINER, P., KRAMER, L., and ALLWAY, T. (Eds) *Communication and Affect: Language and Thought*. London: Academic Press.

LOVAAS, O.I., FREITAG, L., NELSON, K. and WHALEN, C. (1967). 'The establishment of imitation and its use for the establishment of complex behavior in schizophrenic children', *Behavior Research and Therapy*, **5**, 171–81.

LOVAAS, O.I., FIRESTONE, P., ACKERMAN, A., ALEXANDER, D., PERKINS, M. and YOUNG, D. (1980). *Teaching Developmentally Disabled Children – the ME Book*. Baltimore, Maryland: University Park Press.

LOVAAS, O.I. and BURTON LEAT, R. (1981). Videotapes and Leader's Guide which accompany LOVAAS *et al.* (1980). *Teaching Developmentally Disabled Children – the ME Book*. Baltimore, Maryland: University Park Press.

LUDLOW, J.R. and ALLEN, L.M. (1979). 'The effect of early intervention and pre-school stimulus on the development of the Downs' Syndrome child', *Journal of Mental Deficiency Research*, **23**, 29–44.

LYLE, J.G. (1960). 'The effect of an institutional environment upon the verbal development of imbecile children – the Brooklands residential family unit', *Journal of Mental Deficiency Research*, **4**, 14–23.

MAULTSBY, M.C. (1975). *Help Yourself to Happiness through Rational Self-Counselling*. Boston: Marlborough House.

MAULTSBY, M.C. (1984). *Rational Behavior Therapy*. Englewood Cliffs, New Jersey: Prentice-Hall Inc.

McCONACHIE, H. (1983). 'Fathers, mothers, siblings: how do they see themselves?' In: MITTLER, P. and McCONACHIE, H. (Eds) *Parents, Professionals and Mentally Handicapped People: Approaches to Partnership*. London: Croom Helm.

McCONKEY, R. (1981). 'Education without Understanding?', *Special Education Forward Trends*, **8**, 3.

McGLYNN, N. (1980). Encouraging speech development in young profoundly mentally handicapped children. Unpublished Master's degree thesis. University of Glasgow.

MEICHENBAUM, D.H. (1974). *Cognitive Behavior Modification*. New Jersey: General Learning Press.

MILLAR, S. (1968). *The Psychology of Play*. London: Penguin.

MILLER, G.A., GALANTER, F. and PRIBRAM, K.H. (1960). *Plans and the Structure of Behavior*. New York: Holt, Rhinehart and Winston.

MINUCHIN, S. (1974). *Families and Family Therapy*. London: Tavistock Publications.

MITTLER, P. and McCONACHIE, H. (Eds) (1983). *Parents, Professionals and Mentally Handicapped People*. London: Croom Helm.

MOORHEAD. (1982). 'Getting rid of depression with talk and sympathy'. *The Times*, 5.1.82.

NATIONAL SOCIETY FOR MENTALLY HANDICAPPED CHILDREN and NATIONAL SPASTICS SOCIETY (undated). Mentally handicapped children growing up – the Brooklands Experiment. (16mm film).

NELSON, K. (1973). Structure and Strategy in Learning to Talk. Monographs of the Society for Research in Child Development, 38 (1–2 Serial No. 149).

NEWSON, E. (1980). 'Parents as a resource in diagnosis and assessment'. In: OPPE, T. and WOODFORD, P. (Eds) *Early Management of Handicapping Disorders*. IRMMH (Institute of Research into Mental and Multiple Handicap) Reviews of Research and Practice. Amsterdam: Associated Scientific Publishers.

NEWSON, E. and HIPGRAVE, T. (1982). *Getting Through to your Handicapped Child*. Cambridge: Cambridge University Press.

NEWSON, J. (1976). 'Dialogue and development'. In: LOCK, A. (Ed) *Action, Gesture and Symbol: the Emergence of Language*. London: Academic Press.

NIELSEN, L. (1979). *The Comprehending Hand*. National Board of Social Welfare, Kristeneberg 6, Post Box 2555, 2100, Copenhagen O, Denmark. Tel: 01299122.

NIXON, C. (1976). *Exploratory Testing of a Procedural Guide as a Possible Job and for the Health Services*. Wessex Health Care Evaluation Research Team Research Report. University of Southampton: Health Care Evaluation Research Team.

O'DELL, S., (1974). 'Training parents in behaviour modification', *Psychological Bulletin*, **81**, 418–33.

PALMER, C.F. (1984). The Willows Portage microcomputer project. Unpublished MSc dissertation, University of Southampton. In preparation.

PALMER, C.F. and HUGGETT, S.A. (1984). 'Managing the curriculum with a micro'. Paper presented at the 1984 British Psychological Society Division of Educational and Child Psychologists (DECP) Refresher Course, Southampton, England.

PAPERT, S. (1980). *Mindstorms: Children, Computers and Powerful Ideas*. Brighton: The Harvester Press.

PERKINS, E.A. and POWELL, M. (1983). *Asian Families with a Pre-school Handicapped Child*. Study done for West Birmingham Health Authority and Birmingham Inner City Partnership (in Press).

PHILIPS, C.J. and SMITH, B. (1979). 'Service to families of severely educationally handicapped children', *Apex Journal of British Institute of Mental Handicap*, **7**, 1, 28–30.

PHILPS, C. (1984). *Elizabeth Joy*. Tring: Lion Publishing.

PIETERSE, M. and TRELOAR, R. (1981). *Down's Syndrome Program*. Progress Report 1981. Australia: Macquarie University.

PLOWDEN REPORT. GREAT BRITAIN. DEPARTMENT OF EDUCATION AND SCIENCE. CENTRAL ADVISORY COUNCIL FOR EDUCATION (ENGLAND) (1967). *Children and their Primary Schools*. London: HMSO.

POULTON, G. (1974). Educational home visiting in England. Unpublished M.A. dissertation, Southampton University.

POULTON, G., and COUZENS, L. (1981). *Scope for Parents and Children: year 5*. Southampton: University of Southampton.

PUGH, G. (1981). 'The Wessex Portage Project'. In: PUGH, G. (ed) *Parents as Partners: Intervention Schemes and Group Work with Parents of Handicapped Children*. London: National Children's Bureau.

PUGH, G. (Ed) (1981). *Parents as Partners*. London: National Children's Bureau.

READER, L. (1984). 'Pre-school intervention programmes: a review', *Child: Care, Health and Development*, **10**, 4, 237–51.

REVILL, S. and BLUNDEN, R. (1979). 'A home training service for pre-school developmentally handicapped children', *Behaviour Research and Therapy*, **17**, 3, 207–14.

REVILL, S. and BLUNDEN, R. (1980). *A Manual for Implementing a Portage Home Training Service for Developmentally Handicapped Pre-school Children*. Windsor: NFER-NELSON.

REYNELL, J.K. (1973). 'Planning treatment programmes: pre-school children'. In: MITTLER, P. (Ed) *Assessment for Learning in the Mentally Handicapped*. London: Churchill-Livingstone.

RUBISSOW, J., JONES, J. and BRIMBLECOMBE, F. (1979). 'Handicapped children and their families: their use of available services and their unmet needs'. In: NUFFIELD PROVINCIAL HOSPITALS TRUST *Mixed Communications: Problems and Progress in Medical Care, No. 12*. Oxford: University Press.

RUSSELL, P. (1983). 'The parents' perspective of family needs and how to meet them'. In: MITTLER, P. and McCONACHIE, H. (Eds) *Parents, Professionals and Mentally Handicapped People: Approaches to Partnership*. London: Croom Helm.

SANDOW, S. and CLARKE, A.D.B. (1978). 'Home intervention with parents of severely subnormal pre-school children: an interim report', *Child: Care, Health and Development*, **4**, 29–39.

SANDOW, S., CLARKE, A.D.B., COX M.V. and STEWART, R.L. (1981). 'Home intervention with parents of severely subnormal pre-school children: a final report', *Child: Care, Health and Development*, **7**, 3, 135–44.

SCHORTINGHUIS, N. and FROHMAN, A. (1974). 'A comparison of professional paraprofessional success with preschool children', *Journal of Learning Disabilities*, **17**, 245–7.

SCHWARTZ, A. and GOLDIAMOND, I. (1975). *Social Casework: a Behavioural Approach*. New York: Columbia University Press.

SHEARER, M.S. and SHEARER, D. (1972). 'The Portage project: a model for early childhood education', *Exceptional Children*, **39**, 210–17.

SKINNER, B.F. (1969). *Contingencies of Reinforcement: A Theoretical Analysis*. New York: Appleton.

SMITH, J., KUSHLICK, A. and GLOSSOP, C. (1977). *The Wessex Portage Project: A Home Teaching Service for Families with a Pre-School Mentally Handicapped Child*. Research Project No. 125. Part I: The Report, Part II: The Appendices. Available from Wessex Health Care Evaluation Research Team (HCERT) 45–47, Salisbury Road, The University, Highfield, Southampton SO9 5NH.

STEVENS, T. (1981). 'Language matters: 3 – my word!', *Mental Handicap* (formerly *Apex*), **8**, 4, 119.

STEVENSON, J. and GRAHAM, P. (1978). 'Parental reaction to birth of a handicapped child'. *British Journal of Psychiatry*, **132**, 105.

STOKES, T.F. and BAER, D.M. (1977). 'An implicit technology of generalization', *Journal of Applied Behavior Analysis*, **10**, 349–368.

STRATFORD, R.J. and CAMERON, R.J. (1979). 'Aiming at larger targets', British Psychological Society (Division of Educational and Child Psychologists) *DECP Occasional Papers*, **3**, 2, 22–37.

TAYLOR REPORT (1977). *A New Partnership for our Schools*. London: HMSO.

TERDAL, L.E., JACKSON, R.H. and GARNER, A.M. (1976). 'Mother-child interactions: a comparison between normal and developmentally delayed groups'. In: MASH, E.J., HAMMERLYNCK, L.A. and HARDY, L.C. (Eds) *Behavior Modification and Families*. New York: Brunner/Mazel.

TEW, B.J., RAWNSLEY, K., LAWRENCE, K.M. and PAYNE, H. (1977). 'Mental stability following the birth of a child with spina bifida', *British Journal of Psychiatry*, **131**, 79–82.

THOMAS, E.D. and WALTER, C.L. (1973). 'Guidelines for behavioural practice in the open community agency', *Behaviour Research and Therapy*, 11, 193–205.

TIZARD, J. (1961). 'The Brooklands experimental unit', *Nursing Times*, 11 August 61, 1028–30.

TURNER, J. (1980). *Made for Life: Coping, Competence and Cognition*. London: Methuen.

WALKER, M. (1980). *Line Drawing Illustrations for the Revised Makaton Vocabulary*. Surrey: Makaton Vocabulary Development Project.

WARNOCK REPORT. GREAT BRITAIN. DEPARTMENT OF EDUCATION AND SCIENCE. (1978). *Special Educational Needs*. London: HMSO.

WESTMACOTT, E.V.S. and CAMERON, R.J. (1981). *Behaviour Can Change*. London: Macmillan.

WHITE, M. and EAST, K. (1983). *The Wessex Revised Portage Language Checklist*. Windsor: NFER-NELSON.

WISHART, M.C., BIDDER, R.T. and GRAY, O.P. (1980). 'Parental responses to their developmentally delayed children and the South Glamorgan Home Advisory Service', *Child: Care, Health and Development*, **6**, 361–76.

WOLFENDALE, S. (1983). *Parental Participation in Children's Development and Education*. New York: Gordon and Breach.

WOLFENSBERGER, W. and KURTZ, R.A. (1974). 'Use of retardation-related diagnostic and descriptive labels by parents of retarded children', *Journal of Special Education*, **8**, 2, 131–42.

YULE, W. (1975). 'Teaching psychological principles to non-psychologists; training parents in child management', *Journal of Association of Educational Psychologists*.

YULE W. and CARR, J. (Eds) (1981). *Behaviour Modification for the Mentally Handicapped*. London: Croom Helm.

ZETTLE, R.D. and HAYES, S.C. (1980). 'Conceptual and empirical status of rational emotive therapy'. In: HERSEN, M., EISLER, R.M. and MILLER, P.M. (Eds) *Progress in Behavior Modification (Vol 9)*. New York: Academic Press.